DUCK HUNTER
SHOOTS ANGEL

BY **MITCH ALBOM**

★

★

DRAMATISTS
PLAY SERVICE
INC.

DUCK HUNTER SHOOTS ANGEL
Copyright © 2008, Mitch Albom

All Rights Reserved

SPECIAL NOTE
Anyone receiving permission to produce DUCK HUNTER SHOOTS ANGEL is required to give credit to the Author as sole and exclusive Author of the Play on the title page of all programs distributed in connection with performances of the Play and in all instances in which the title of the Play appears for purposes of advertising, publicizing or otherwise exploiting the Play and/or a production thereof. The name of the Author must appear on a separate line, in which no other name appears, immediately beneath the title and in size of type equal to 50% of the size of the largest, most prominent letter used for the title of the Play. No person, firm or entity may receive credit larger or more prominent than that accorded the Author. The following acknowledgment must appear on the title page in all programs distributed in connection with performances of the Play:

Commissioned by and premiered by
The Purple Rose Theatre Company.

SPECIAL NOTE ON SONGS AND RECORDINGS
For performances of copyrighted songs, arrangements or recordings mentioned in this Play, the permission of the copyright owner(s) must be obtained. Other songs, arrangements or recordings may be substituted provided permission from the copyright owner(s) of such songs, arrangements or recordings is obtained; or songs, arrangements or recordings in the public domain may be substituted.

DUCK HUNTER SHOOTS ANGEL received its world premiere by The Purple Rose Theatre Company (Jeff Daniels, Executive Director; Guy Sanville, Artistic Director; Alan Ribant, Managing Director) in Chelsea, Michigan, opening on November 18, 2006. It was directed by Guy Sanville; the set design was by Steve Klein; the lighting design was by Reid Johnson; the costume design was by Christianne Myers; the sound design was by Quintessa Duffield; and the production stage manager was Michelle Didomenico. The cast was as follows:

PHIL .... Randolph Fitzpatrick
SANDY .... James Krag
THE VOICE .... Grant R. Krause
LESTER .... Ryan Carlson
DUANE .... Wayne David Parker
DUWELL .... Joseph Albright
LENNY .... Wallace Bridges
WOMAN .... Jenny McKnight
KANSAS .... Jessica Cloud

CHARACTERS

SANDY — late 30s/40ish, tabloid journalist

LENNY — African American, 30s, photographer

LESTER — 30s, publisher of tabloid

DUANE — late 30s, short, Southern, duck hunter

DUWELL — his brother, bigger, late 30s, Southern, duck hunter

WOMAN — late 20s, Southern

KANSAS — teenager, 17

VOICE/BANK LOAN OFFICER — male, late 40s

GATOR MAN CREATURE — a half man/half alligator

PLACE

Various at various times: a swamp in Alabama; a convenience store in Alabama; a supermarket tabloid's office.

TIME

Now.

SET

One large sprawling tree sits in the center of the stage. Depending on size, a hole can be cut in its trunk, allowing actors to enter and exit through it.

DUCK HUNTER SHOOTS ANGEL

ACT ONE

Lights up on a giant tree. Leaning against it, reading a book, is a large creature, with a man's body and an alligator head. The sounds of crickets and swamp noise are interrupted by the sudden blast of gunfire. The creature looks to the sky, then returns to his book as the gunfire subsides. (Note: As the play continues, actors will come on and off stage from different angles, overlapping scenes.) Enter Sandy, a journalist, carrying a coffee cup. He nods at the creature: It leaps to its feet, dances around him. Sandy takes a sip as if this is normal behavior, chuckles a little. Then, as if forgetting his manners, offers the Beast a sip.

SANDY. Mmmph. I'm sorry. Want some? *(The Beast declines. Keeps dancing. Sandy shrugs.)* Suit yourself.
VOICE. *(Offstage, as if from top/rear of the theater.)* So, what is it that you do, Sandy?
SANDY. *(Turning to the voice.)* Do? I'm a writer.
VOICE. What do you write?
SANDY. Crap. I write crap. *(Back to the creature.)* You sure you don't want some? I can make decaf. *(The creature defers. Sandy back to voice:)*
VOICE. You said you wrote —
SANDY. Crap. Yeah.
VOICE. Explain.
SANDY. Explain crap? Well. If I had a dictionary — *(Gator Man quickly produces dictionary, holds it open.)* Ah. Let's see ... Crap. One. Nonsense. Drivel. Two. A lie. An exaggeration. Three. Rubbish. Junk. As in, "Will you clean up that crap?" *(Closing*

book.) Well, no. You see. That was the problem. I wouldn't clean it up. I just made more of it. When the old crap went dry, I made up new crap. I was a crap recycler. I should have had a red plastic bin outside my office door: "Crap."

VOICE. Tell me about the angel.

SANDY. But you asked me what I do. I write crap — because I'm *supposed* to write crap. For a supermarket tabloid, called *The Weekly World and Globe*. It's not even a *good* tabloid. It's like ten notches BELOW the *National Enquirer*. You know how hard *that* is to pull off? *(Creature shrugs. As Sandy talks, it performs numerous tasks.)*

VOICE. Tell me about the Angel, Sandy —

SANDY. It's not that I didn't have higher aspirations. I mean, honestly. *(Picks up tabloid from desk.)* Does anyone grow UP wanting to write for the *Weekly World and Globe*? Think about that name: The World and Globe? Shouldn't one word be enough for that? And here's the kicker. *The Weekly World and Globe*? It comes out *twice a week!* They were gonna call it the *BI-Weekly World and Globe*, but the owners thought that sounded gay. Or Bi. Not that our readers would know the difference. We sell four hundred thousand copies each week — twice a week — and I fill the pages. I write about aliens taking over the White House and three-headed babies who speak three languages. I give them half-boy-half-wolf creatures that hide inside shopping carts at the Piggly Wiggly. I give them ... *(As if realizing he hasn't acknowledged the creature's existence until now, Sandy points to it.)* "Man, eaten by alligator, comes back in alligator's body, takes revenge on swamp." You wouldn't believe how well that story sold. *(To Beast.)* You can go now. *(Beast strikes a scary pose.)* No, really. Go. *(Another scary pose.)* BEGONE, BEAST! BACK TO THE SWAMP THAT SPAWNED YOU! *(A flash of lightning. A thunder clap. Both Sandy and Beast look up, as if to say: Where did THAT come from?)* No, really, Phil. We're done. Take off the costume and leave it in the studio. *(The Beast stalks off, dejected.)* You asked me what I do. This is what I do: I write crap, for the *Weekly World and Globe*, which comes out twice a week. I don't do it for art. I don't do it for satisfaction. I do it for this. *(Enter Lester, holding an envelope. He hands it to Sandy then turns upstage and begins preening as if looking in a mirror.)* My paycheck. Which comes out once a week.

VOICE. The Angel?

SANDY. OK. OK. One day I get called into the boss's office. He says —

LESTER and SANDY. "Sandy, I've got something you're gonna love."

SANDY. Lester, I don't love anything you're gonna give me.

LESTER. C'mon. Everyone loves something. I love my spread sheets. I love the Porsche 930. I love two girls at once. Well ... I will once I try it.

SANDY. *(To audience.)* He's very young. Also very rich. His Dad started the *Weekly World and Globe*, then died of a heart attack. At his desk. Actually ON his desk. Actually, on his *secretary*, who was on his desk.

LESTER. I miss Dad.

SANDY. I wrote the obituary: "We, the staff at the *Weekly World and Globe*, mourn the passing of our leader and founder, Horton J. Bryce, but comfort ourselves knowing that he is dining with Elvis, Princess Di, and Amelia Earhart." See photo page five.

LESTER. *(Moved.)* That's beautiful.

SANDY. That's what I do.

LESTER. Sandy, I've got something you're gonna love.

SANDY. So we're back to that —

LESTER. A call comes in this morning. From Alabama. Says he only wants to talk to us.

SANDY. We're the paper of record in Alabama.

LESTER. Says he was out hunting when he heard a bang.

SANDY. A bang when hunting? Imagine that.

LESTER. Then the strangest sound. Like an opera singer.

SANDY. They shot Pavarotti!

LESTER. A woman. But wait. That's not a bad idea ... *(Grabs small tape recorder. Talks into it.)* Pavarotti shot ... *(He eyeballs Sandy, looking for inspiration.)* ... by Big FOOT! That'll be next week's cover.

SANDY. Wait. Did you say Alabama?

LESTER. I said Big Foot.

SANDY. You said Alabama. I am not going down there.

LESTER. Why not?

SANDY. Well, for one thing, every time I go down south, I break out.

LESTER. Hives?

SANDY. Righteousness. I see poverty, racism, ignorance.

LESTER. You live in New York. You can see that in your lobby.

7

SANDY. Next thing you know, I want to write about injustice, progressive thought —

LESTER. *(Yawning loudly for effect.)* Yawning! I'm yaww-ning!

SANDY. Social activism, the legacy of the civil rights movement —

LESTER. Aw, who gives a rat's ass?

SANDY. Precisely! *(Softer.)* Precisely ... And I don't give a rat's ass either. No South. Especially not Alabama.

LESTER. Don't be such a snob. You worked there when you were younger. When you were —

SANDY. Legitimate?

LESTER. I was gonna say broke. Why do people confuse the two? *(Mocking.)* "Oh, when I was poor, I was legitimate. I was an artist. But now that I have money, I'm shit." You think Warren Buffet says that? You think JIMMY Buffet says that? Why can't earning money make you legitimate? American Express thinks so.

SANDY. American Express?

LESTER. Yeah. You're poor, you get no card. "Go away, little broke person." But you make a little dough, you get a green card. You make a little more, you get a gold card. You make A LOT more you get — ta-da! — platinum. "Right this way, Lester, your massage table is ready." I love it. Color-coded legitimacy. Lets you know where you stand in life. *(As he finishes, the creature leaps onto the stage, trying to be scary.)* What's up, Phil?

SANDY. Yeah, well, I'm not going to Alabama.

LESTER. So anyhow, you're gonna love this.

SANDY. You're not listen —

LESTER. This guy hears a bang, and then the opera singer sound, and then a big thing falls from the sky.

SANDY. I gotta go —

LESTER. He scrambles through the woods, and there he sees it, off in the distance, face down in a lake.

SANDY. *(Turning to leave.)* Goodbye, Lester.

LESTER. Take a guess.

SANDY. *(As he walks away.)* A spaceship.

LESTER. Better.

SANDY. Big Foot.

LESTER. *(Gleeful.)* Better. *(The Beast jumps out front, arms open, as if presenting himself.)*

SANDY. *(Staring.)* Half-man, half-alligator?

LESTER. An angel. *(Sandy stops, intrigued against his better judg-*

8

ment.)

SANDY. Right.

LESTER. *(Cooing.)* An aaaangel.

SANDY. I'm not going south.

LESTER. Come on. It's right up your alley. You're anti-gun, anti-redneck, and I KNOW you don't believe in a higher power.

SANDY. How would *you* know that?

LESTER. You're working here, aren't you?

SANDY. Don't remind me.

LESTER. And take Lumpy with you.

SANDY. His name is Lenny. And what for? He's a photographer. You think an angel wants its picture taken?

LESTER. Take some money. Pay it off.

SANDY. It doesn't need money.

LESTER. Take the Platinum card.

SANDY. It's an ANGEL!

LESTER. *(As if Sandy is pathetic and the game is over.)* What the hell's the matter with you? There's no angel. Take some money to pay whatever rednecks cooked this up and get 'em to sell it to us and not the *Enquirer*. Get some pictures, too, redneck hunters and anything dressed in an angel costume.

SANDY. Why don't you just simulate it in the studio?

LESTER. Those arty-farts? They'll want to hire eight models and a catering crew. Besides, this justifies the travel budget. Take my "home boy" Lumpy.

SANDY. Lenny. I am not going south.

LESTER. You're going and that's that.

SANDY. *(Back to voice.)* And that was that. *(Exit Sandy and Lester. Lights up on Duwell and Duane, in the swamp, sitting back-to-back, holding rifles.)*

DUANE. *(Forlornly.)* And that's that.

DUWELL. I cain't believe we shot it.

DUANE. I had so many plans.

DUWELL. I cain't believe we shot it.

DUANE. I was gonna get a double-wide. For Christmas. For me and Jo-leen. For Christmas. Not this Christmas, but, you know, some Christmas.

DUWELL. I cain't believe we shot it.

DUANE. *(Annoyed.)* Would you mind sayin' something else, please?

DUWELL. *(Thinks for a moment.)* I cain't believe you shot it.

DUANE. ME? How d'ya know I shot it? Your gun was firin', too!

DUWELL. You're a better shot than me.

DUANE. Hell, I know that! But how d'ya know I shot it?

DUWELL. I'm givin' you a compliment.

DUANE. No thank you! No thank you, I say! I don't need no compliment that's gonna send me straight to the gates of hell! I ain't so good a shot that I could hit one of God's heavenly creatures! Seems to me a shot like that could only come in the most haphazard of firin's, like the firin's of a man who is completely clueless as to the ways of a shotgun and therefore, through sheer blind coincidence, he brings down a creature that under normal circumstances could avoid any *predictable* bullet from any *predictable* gunman, exceptin' the type who drank a fifth of Jack Daniels before he come out to hunt ... In other words, YOU shot it.

DUWELL *(Pauses, thinks this over.)* I cain't believe we shot it. *(Sounds of a distant howl, woman's voice, haunting.)*

DUANE. Oh, Jesus.

DUWELL. I don't think it's Jesus. It had blond hair, remember?

DUANE. That sound. What have you done, Duwell?

DUWELL. Quit sayin' it was me, Duane!

DUANE. It's the end of the world thing. Arma-whatever.

DUWELL. Armagetcha.

DUANE. Armagetcha.

DUWELL. I cain't believe we shot it.

DUANE. SHUT THE HELL UP!

DUWELL. Don't say "hell." It might hear you. *(Exit Duane and Duwell. Lights up on Sandy and Lenny, driving.)*

LENNY. I didn't hear you.

SANDY. What?

LENNY. At least I *hope* I didn't hear you. I thought you said somebody shot an angel.

SANDY. I did. That's where we're going. An angel. Somebody shot one.

LENNY. Did they kill it — or wound it?

SANDY. It's Alabama. They probably gave it an NRA membership. Didn't Lester tell you where you were going on this assignment?

LENNY. Lester don't talk to me. He don't even know my name. He sends a message to my pager. "Hey, hey, home boy. Gotta gig for you." A gig? Whadda I look like, Miles Davis?

SANDY. "Home boy"?

10

LENNY. Yeah, like we did a drive-by together. I live in the *suburbs!*
SANDY. Why don't you stand up to him?
LENNY. 'Cause he's a slimy, condescending, trust-fund baby peckerhead. *(Exhale.)* And I need the money.
SANDY. Well, I need a beer … *(Squinting out window.)* There's bound to be someplace in the next five hundred miles. How 'bout you? You hungry?
LENNY. Yeah. I got a blood sugar thing.
SANDY. You're diabetic? Why didn't you say something?
LENNY. I ain't diabetic. I got a blood sugar thing. I like sugar; it's in my blood. My Daddy was a baker. Made Boston cream pies, French éclairs …
SANDY. Wow.
LENNY. Yeah, well, white folks bought that shit. We ate donuts.
SANDY. Too bad.
LENNY. Too bad, my ass. I *love* donuts! Nothing like a donut dipped in chocolate milk to start your day out right.
SANDY. *(Pointing at road sign.)* In that case, Gasmart five miles ahead.
LENNY. My mother used to talk about them.
SANDY. Donuts?
LENNY. Angels. She knew all the different ones.
SADNY; There are different angels?
LENNY. Oh, yeah. They ain't all little midgets floating around with harps and shit.
SANDY. Harps and shit?
LENNY. There's loads of different angels. Guardian Angels, Cherubim, Seraphim, archangels, dark angels, angels that watch over wind, angels that watch over fire.
SANDY. I don't believe in angels.
LENNY. *(Mock horror.)* Uhhhh! Don't say that while you're driving! Ain't you never heard of the car fairy?
SANDY. Come on. Really. All these sad people thinking their lives are being guided by some divine force? It's pathetic. Especially down here. The "Bible Belt." It sounds like something they sell at the Gap. "Let me slip on my Bible Belt. Then I'll do my Bible buckle. That'll hold up my Bible pants."
LENNY. And what do you believe guides people's lives?
SANDY. … Mistakes.
LENNY. Mistakes.

SANDY. That's right. Mistakes. There's no plan. There's no "holy" force field. Life is about stumbling from one mistake into the other, like someone pushed you down the stairs. You get your hands up. You protect your vital parts. But down you go, bump, bump, bump, 'til you die.

LENNY. *(A pause.)* You on medication?

SANDY. I hate the south.

LENNY. Didn't you work down here?

SANDY. For a while. A small daily in Birmingham.

LENNY. Why'd you leave?

SANDY. Look around.

LENNY. I don't see nothin'.

SANDY. Precisely. I wanted to see something.

LENNY. What?

SANDY. The world. Some drama. I wanted to be a hot shot reporter. So I did this investigative story. Police corruption in a backwater town. It won an award. I got offers. I went north.

LENNY. Left all this, huh?

SANDY. It wasn't a hard decision. Not really. *(Looks off, something gnawing at him.)*

LENNY. Not really?

SANDY. *(Coming back.)* Huh?

LENNY. Seemed like you were about to say something else.

SANDY. No. Nothing else. *(Lights up on Woman.)*

WOMAN. *(Playfully, to Sandy.)* What else? *(Sandy rises to her, in memory moment.)*

SANDY. What do you mean, what else? *(He sounds younger, less jaded. He absentmindedly scratches his neck and taps his foot.)* No, really, what do you mean "what else"?

WOMAN. Well, whenever you got some surprise you kinda scratch your neck. *(He stops scratching his neck.)* And your foot taps like you had too much coffee. *(He stops tapping his foot.)*

SANDY. How did you pick that up so fast? We've only been going out, what …

WOMAN. Ten months, two weeks, four days, six hours, give or take.

SANDY. Give or take what?

WOMAN. Daylight Savings … I keep a diary. I figure you oughta always have someone to talk to, even if it is yourself.

SANDY. How did I get involved with a Southern girl?

WOMAN. You came south, remember? *(Sandy takes her in his*

arms, happily.)
SANDY. Oh, yeah. That's what that moving truck was all about.
WOMAN. *(Happy.)* So what is it?
SANDY. Welll … That investigative piece I've been working on? It's going front page tomorrow. Above the fold!
WOMAN. That's GREAT, Sandy! … What's the fold?
SANDY. In the newspaper. You know. Where they bend it?
WOMAN. Well, you deserve it. You worked like a madman.
SANDY. Let's go celebrate somewhere. How about chili dogs?
WOMAN. And French fries!
LENNY. *(Loudly.)* And Ovaltine!
SANDY. *(Turning back.)* What? *(Woman exits.)*
LENNY. Ovaltine! That's what I could go for! Donuts and Ovaltine! Like I said, I got a blood sugar thing.
SANDY. *(Settling back into moment.)* In that case, Gasmart three miles. Can you make it? *(Lights off on them, lights up on Duane and Duwell, making their way through the woods, rifles in hands.)*
DUANE. Duwell, I ain't gonna make it! Listen to my heart beat! Bump, bump, bump, bump. I'm liable to have a corollary.
DUWELL. Calm down, now, Duane. We'll figure some way outa this.
DUANE. There ain't no way out, Duwell. Less'n you think you can outrun the Lord.
DUWELL. Maybe it healed itself.
DUANE. Healed itself?
DUWELL. The angel. You know. Maybe it just looked at the wound and closed it up like them Terminator movies.
DUANE. You oughtn't be comparing the Lord's angels to the Terminator, Duwell!
DUWELL. I wasn't comparing, Duane! I was holding up one against the other. *(Duane looks. Isn't that comparing?)* Anyhow, it happens all the time. Lookit this. In the *Weekly World and Globe.* *(He pulls copy from his knapsack. Points to story.)*
DUANE. *(Reading.)* Injured fireman heals himself, saves nun from fire.
DUWELL. You see?
DUANE. *(Skeptical.)* Says he broke both legs, both arms, his neck and his spine, but when he saw the nun, he ran up the stairs and saved her.
DUWELL. Miracles happen.

DUANE. It's next to a story about a four-headed cow.

DUWELL. I read that. Four heads, but only three udders. Strange.

DUANE. *(Turning page.)* Look. Barbara Bush is pregnant ... And Elvis is the father.

DUWELL. Uh-oh.

DUANE. *(Spinning, rifle drawn.)* Uh-oh, what? UH-OH, WHAT?

DUWELL. *(Gently lowering tip of Duane's rifle with his finger. He leans down and picks up a white feather.)* Uh-oh *this.*

DUANE. *(Nervous.)* Aw, now, how do you know that's ... I mean, how do you know? ... That could be from a duck. *(Duwell holds the feather up high. A burst of thunder. A clap of lighting.)* Or maybe not.

DUWELL. *(Scared witless.)* Now what, Duane?

DUANE. Now what, Duwell? *(Lights off on them: back up on Lenny and Sandy.)*

LENNY. Then what, Sandy?

SANDY. Then what what?

LENNY. You didn't finish. After you left here. You sure as shit didn't leave to join the *World and Globe.*

SANDY. No, no. I was legitimate — for a while. Big city paper. Big headlines. Big stories.

LENNY. Big time.

SANDY. But my paycheck wasn't. Not big enough.

LENNY. C'mon, man. I heard them papers pay well. How much you need anyhow?

SANDY. I bet.

LENNY. *(Confused.)* You bet what?

SANDY. I bet on anything that had a score.

LENNY. *(Getting it.)* Ahh. You got in over your head.

SANDY. It wasn't hard. I was single. I liked the image, you know? Drink, smoke, lay down a few bets, like those Damon Runyan newspaper types? A few bad horses. A few bad football games. It's so damn ... seductive. There is nothing so sure as a bet that hasn't been proven wrong ... until it is. Anyhow, it got bad. I needed dough. I did something I shouldn't have done. And then I get called in.

LENNY. Called in?

SANDY. The executive editor. You know how they are. Sit down, Sandy. We need to talk." *(Lenny assumes posture and tone as if he is Sandy.)*

LENNY. Talk about what?

SANDY. The cops picked up that numbers guy, Delouca.

14

LENNY. Yeah, so?

SANDY. He had your name in his books.

LENNY. Oh, come on.

SANDY. Did you borrow money from him?

LENNY. Oh, come on.

SANDY. You know our ethics policy.

LENNY. Oh, come on.

SANDY. Do you have a problem, Sandy? *(Lenny comes out of it, back to himself.)*

LENNY. *Did* you have a problem, Sandy?

SANDY. *(Beat. Mimics Lenny.)* Oh, come on. *(Beat.)* They let me go. Told me I needed help. I did need help. But what I really needed was money. *(Enter Lester.)*

LESTER. We have money.

SANDY. *(Turning.)* How much money?

LESTER. More than those losers in the "legitimate" press are paying you. My father says you're a real reporter.

SANDY. I *was* a real reporter.

LESTER. Twice your pay. Half the work.

SANDY. What do I do? *(Enter Half Man/Half Alligator, leaping onto stage.)*

LESTER. You do him. Twice your pay.

SANDY. *(Resigned.)* Twice my pay.

LESTER. What do you say?

LENNY. What did you say?

SANDY. What could I say?

LENNY. Hey what's that?

SANDY. What's what? *(Sandy swerves. Sudden loud sound of wheel thumping. All four actors bounce at the thump.)*

LENNY. Sandy, what did we just hit? *(Blackout. Sound of gunshots. Lights up on Duane and Duwell, entering with guns high, moving in slow motion as if hunting. Both seem completely inept, firing wildly, looking to sky as they tumble and fire some more. Finally they snap out of it into real time motion. They are giddy with success.)*

DUANE. Duwell, I think we hit something!

DUWELL. We put enough ammo up there!

DUANE. WHOOO-EE! We finally got us a mallard! *(They dance around each other.)*

DUWELL. YESS! YESS!

DUANE. They ain't gonna laugh at us no more now, Duwell!

DUWELL. YESS! YESS!

DUANE. OUR FIRST DUCK! I'm gonna fry it! No, I'm gonna *deep* fry it!

DUWELL. *(Hands shielding eyes.)* Duane …

DUANE. *(Does the same.)* What the hell?

DUWELL. It's beautiful.

DUANE. It's huge!

DUWELL. No wonder we didn't miss it.

DUANE. It's coming down slow.

DUWELL. It'd be hard to miss THAT.

DUANE. Duwell?

DUWELL. Duane? … That ain't a duck is it? *(Sounds of angel's plaintive voice.)*

DUANE. I don't believe so, Duwell. *(Both drop their rifles in total shock.)* Holy mother Mary!

DUWELL. RUN!

DUANE. HOLY MOTHER MARY AND JESUS!

DUWELL. *(Running away.)* What did we hit? *(The sounds of something falling, then a loud thump and splash. Duane and Duwell fall to their knees. Lights up on Sandy and Lenny.)*

LENNY. What did we hit?

SANDY. I don't know. It's so damn dark. I think it was a dead animal.

LENNY. Ain't you gonna go back and look?

SANDY. I thought you said you were hungry.

LENNY. Yeah, so?

SANDY. So we're going to the Gasmart. It's a quarter mile ahead. *(Lenny gives him a look.)* Look, there are dead animals all over these southern highways. What are we gonna do? Take it home and rehab it?

LENNY. So you just leave it there to die?

SANDY. What? You never stepped on an ant before? And you left it there to die?

LENNY. *(Sighing.)* You're cold, man.

SANDY. *(Cynically.)* Yeah, I'm a cold man. *(As if pulling into the Gasmart.)* And here's your cold chocolate milk and donuts place. The Gasmart … Nice sign.

LENNY. Which one?

SANDY. That one. "Eat Here, Get Gas."

LENNY. *(Slight laugh.)* Alabama.

SANDY. Alabama *(Lights up on Lester and Gator Man, who is measuring him like a tailor as he speaks.)*

LESTER. *(On phone.)* Alabama? ... the Comfort Inn ... What city? I don't know. How many cities they got in Alabama? ... That many? Really? Wow ... Try the southern ones ... I'll hold. *(To Gator.)* Can you believe this? You know that duck-hunters-shoot-angel story I sent Sandy and Lumpy on? I'm eating lunch with Josetti from CNN, and somewhere during his fourth scotch he tells me they've got a crew in Alabama, chasing some rumor about an angel being shot down over a lake. I nearly wet myself. I gotta get ahold of Sandy. Speed this up. If we get it first, we'll have those pompous TV news pricks looking like they're chasing *us* for once! I could end up on Larry King ... *(As if on show, overdoing it.)* Hello, Larry ... Hellloo, Larry ... Hello, Lar — *(Back to phone.)* Hello? Huh? Have you found that Comfort Inn yet, lady? ... Thirty-six Comfort Inns? ... *(Scrambling through papers on desk.)* ... Gimme the one closest to ... Telulah County ... Yeah. That's right. Te-lu-lah. Am I talking too fast for you? ... *(To Beast.)* ... Southern folks. They sleep with their sisters ... Hello? ... *(He's been hung up on.)* ... HELLO? HELLO? *(Exit Lester and Creature. Lights up on Duane and Duwell, as if mucking through marsh. Sound of crickets.)*

DUANE. Hello? Anybody out there?

DUWELL. Maybe it disappeared.

DUANE. Maybe we imagined the whole thing.

DUWELL. You saw it fall, same as me, Duane.

DUANE. Don't tell me what I saw, Duwell. I ain't been drinking as long as you have.

DUWELL. Lemme refresh your memory. Long, white robe, blond hair, some big old wings.

DUANE. *(Glumly.)* You forgot the glowing part.

DUWELL. Yeah. And she glowed.

DUANE. Oooh, we really stepped in it this time, Duwell. It's hell and damnation.

DUWELL. Hell and damnation?

DUANE. Hell and damnation.

DUWELL. Maybe she's the forgiving type.

DUANE. Oh, sure. You're an angel, and you're floating over the earth, minding your own business, thinking about what song you're gonna play on the harp tonight — and then boom! Somebody blows a twelve-gauge through your belly! I'm sure forgiveness is the first thing on your mind!

DUWELL. Maybe she drown-ded.

DUANE. Don't be an idiot.

DUWELL. Why am I an idiot?

DUANE. I been wondering that for years.

DUWELL. She coulda drown-ded.

DUANE. She couldn't have "drown-ded," Duwell. She's an angel. Angels don't drown.

DUWELL. They don't get shot, neither.

DUANE. Well that was your doin', not mine.

DUWELL. Look. Out there. Ain't that about where she came down? Mudder's Lake?

DUANE. I don't see no light.

DUWELL. *(Despairingly.)* Me neither. No light. No glow. No sign of life. *(Lights up on Sandy and Lenny.)*

SANDY. Any sign of life in there?

LENNY. *(Stretching neck.)* None I can see.

SANDY. The sign says "Open."

LENNY. Yep. Looks like an old sign, though. *(They sit still for a moment.)*

SANDY. Lenny?

LENNY. Hmm?

SANDY. Are you bothered by being down in the deep south? The whole racial history?

LENNY. Why you ask me that?

SANDY. Well, you're not getting out of the car.

LENNY. Hmmph. Seems to me you the one oughta be bothered by history. My folks was too busy fetchin' your folks' breakfast.

SANDY. Hey, don't look at me. I see everybody the same.

LENNY. Oh, you see everyone the same.

SANDY. Yeah.

LENNY. Nigga, please.

SANDY. *(Pause.)* I never got that.

LENNY. What?

SANDY. How you can say that word and be Black.

LENNY. It's just an expression.

SANDY. An expression?

LENNY. Yeah. Like "I see everyone the same."

SANDY. Hey, wait a min —

LENNY. Lookit, now. No one sees everyone the same. That's 'cause

18

we're all different. And while I may be Black, I am not some ex-slave visiting the plantation. I'm a photographer with a job to do. Even my camera got room for black and white in it without a quarrel.

SANDY. Sorry. I didn't mean to offend you with my openmindedness.

LENNY. Now go in there and get us some food!

SANDY. You're not coming?

LENNY. Are you crazy? I'm a three-hundred-pound Black man in Alabama! These crackers ain't gonna talk to me!

SANDY. I thought you said —

LENNY. I was talkin' to *you!* You one of the *smart* White people! Now get inside before they shoots us for diluting the racial order! *(Sandy jumps out. He starts, stops, then turns back to Lenny, who can't control his laughter.)*

SANDY. You're messing with me.

LENNY *(Laughing hard.)* Sorry, man. You too easy. You got guilt written all over you.

SANDY. I'll go get some donuts, OK, Malcolm? You and the nation of Islam just relax. *(Lenny puts hands behind head, grinning. Lights off on them, Lights up on Duane and Duwell. Duwell is circling around Duane nervously.)*

DUANE. Just relax. Just relax.

DUWELL. *(Almost hyperventilating.)* How can we relax? First we shot an angel, then it drown-ded, now it's a missing person.

DUANE. *(Raising hand.)* Ooh! Ooh! I got an idea! We call Sheriff Otis down at the fish and game office. We tell him, we tell-him, we think-we-think-we-think-we-think we saw hunters shootin' out of season — yeah! Shootin' out of season — and he ought to check it out.

DUWELL. What'll we say they was shootin'?

DUANE. Anything besides ducks. A deer. An elk. A Democrat. As long as it'll get him to come out.

DUWELL. But if he comes out, then he might find the angel.

DUANE. Exactly. He'll find it, and we'll be long gone.

DUWELL. Then what?

DUANE. Then who cares? It's the fish and game's problem.

DUWELL. What if it tells?

DUANE. What if what tells?

DUWELL. The angel? What if it tells on us?

DUANE. *(Mocking.)* "What if it tells on us?" Who's it gonna tell?

19

The teacher? Besides, how's it know it was us?

DUWELL. An angel knows everything.

DUANE. It didn't know enough to get outa the way of your bullet.

DUWELL. It wasn't *my* bullet!

DUANE. Go make the damn phone call, will ya?

DUWELL. Why do I gotta make the call?

DUANE. 'Cause Otis knows me. He'll recognize my voice. Now just call and tell him someone was huntin' out of season and they took down something big. Then hang up. You get it? Don't say nothing about the angel? You get it? *(Lights up on Sandy, center stage, talking to the voice.)*

SANDY. You get it? That's what happened. A phone call was made. Another phone call was made. And Lenny and I were in Alabama, at the "Eat Here, Get Gas" place. I knew it was a waste of time. But there we were. Um … if you don't mind my saying, these are some unusual questions. Do you normally, you know, with first-timers, ask stuff like this?

VOICE. Why didn't you believe it?

SANDY. Believe what? The story? Two oakies plug a heavenly body? Would you buy that?

VOICE. You don't believe in angels.

SANDY. *(Cynically.)* My life has not exactly been Heaven-blessed.

VOICE. You had health?

SANDY. Yeah.

VOICE. You had success?

SANDY. For a while.

VOICE. A wife? A family?

SANDY. *(Beat.)* No … No time.

VOICE. What about love?

SANDY. What about it?

VOICE. Was there nobody special?

SANDY. A girl? You mean a girl, right? Oh, well. There were lots of girls. Plenty of girls. Some girls. Lately there was Janice from the sales department. Before her was Theresa from the gym. Before her was Beth from research, and let's see —

VOICE. Anybody *special?*

SANDY. Special. *(Pause.)* There was one girl. Once. Long time ago. *(Warming.)* She was special. *(Lights up on Woman, she enters smiling, singing Happy Birthday with a candle and small cake.)*

VOICE. And what happened?

SANDY. *(Looking in her eyes.)* I left her behind. I had things I just wanted to accomplish, you know? She couldn't understand that. She just wanted … me. And I couldn't understand that. *(She blows out candle. Exits.)*

VOICE. What happened?

SANDY. I told you. I left her behind. It's no big deal. I was looking for something else. *(Lights up on inside of Gasmart, Kansas behind the counter.)*

KANSAS. Whatcha looking for?

SANDY. Donuts.

KANSAS. Against the wall, in the corner.

SANDY. You got any chocolate milk?

KANSAS. Somebody's got a sweet tooth.

SANDY. Yeah, well that somebody is out in the car. I'm the designated shopper.

VOICE. So did you find what you were looking for?

SANDY. *(To Voice.)* What?

KANSAS. How far along is she?

SANDY. *(To Kansas.)* What?

KANSAS. Your wife?

SANDY. My wife?

KANSAS. The one in the car? She's pregnant, right?

SANDY. Why do you ask that?

VOICE. Did you find what you were looking for?

SANDY. *(To Voice.)* Why do you ask that?

KANSAS. *(Slight giggle.)* 'Cause who else would want donuts and chocolate milk in the middle of the night? She must have cravings. Does she want pickles, too?

SANDY. I'm sorry?

VOICE. What did she want?

SANDY. *(To Voice.)* I don't know what she wanted!

KANSAS. *(Flustered.)* OK. Skip the pickles.

VOICE. And what did you want?

KANSAS. Boy or girl?

SANDY. *(To Voice.)* I wanted something else.

KANSAS. Besides a boy or a girl?

VOICE. And did you get it?

SANDY. *(To Voice.)* I got what I deserve!

KANSAS. I guess that means a boy.

SANDY. *(To Kansas.)* Excuse me?

VOICE. Is that when you stopped believing in angels?

SANDY. *(To Voice.)* I never believed in angels!

KANSAS. Storks.

SANDY. What?

KANSAS. Storks. Storks bring babies. Not angels. You don't believe in storks.

SANDY. *(Shaking this off.)* No. You're right. I don't believe in storks.

KANSAS. Me, neither. Angels are another matter.

SANDY. You believe in angels?

KANSAS. Yes, sir.

SANDY. Have you ever seen one?

KANSAS. Not yet. But you don't have to see something to believe in it, right?

SANDY. You should be working for my paper.

KANSAS. Come again?

SANDY. Listen. Have you ever seen anything "other worldly" by the swamp where they go duck hunting?

KANSAS. *(Giggling.)* Well, you'd have to ask someone who hunts. I don't believe in shooting unarmed creatures.

SANDY. And who hunts around here?

KANSAS. It's more like who doesn't.

SANDY. Any regulars? Guys out there all the time?

KANSAS. Well, that would be any male come hunting season. But if I had to pick, I'd say Duane Early and his brother Duwell. They're both outa work on accounta the economy and also 'cause they don't have any skills. So they mostly hunt.

SANDY. They don't have much money, huh? *(He pulls out wad of bills as Kansas slowly rings up the items on a hand crank register. She notices the money.)*

KANSAS. You obviously aren't from around here.

SANDY. No, I'm not … *(Hesitating.)* … I'm from New York City.

KANSAS. Hmm. Big place, huh?

SANDY. We're not that different from you folks. We just eat faster. And talk faster. And … *(Waiting on her.)* ring up faster. What's your name?

KANSAS. Kansas.

SANDY. Kansas. Like the state.

KANSAS. Boy, New Yorkers really *are* fast.

SANDY. Why Kansas?

KANSAS. My mom. She loved the *Wizard of Oz*. She said she

thought Kansas sounded nice. You know, "no place like home." No place like Kansas. Nobody like *(Pointing to herself.)* Kansas.

SANDY. That's actually sweet. *(Beat.)* I'm shocked. *(Beat.)* Did your mom ever go there?

KANSAS. My Mom never left Alabama.

SANDY. What did sh — *(Honking sound from car.)*

KANSAS. Sounds like the little misses is hungry.

SANDY. Believe me, there's nothing "little" or "misses" about him.

KANSAS. *Him?*

SANDY. Listen, Kansas, did you ever see anyone around here dress up as an angel? Halloween? Christmas? Someone who might keep an angel costume around?

KANSAS. They do a pageant every year down at the Church.

SANDY. And those hunters' names again?

KANSAS. Duane and Duwell?

SANDY. Duane and Duwell. *(Lights up on Duane and Duwell, crickets and water sounds. Duwell walking arms out as if balancing on a log.)*

DUWELL. Duane and Duwell, goin to hell ... Duane and Duwell, goin to hell —

DUANE. Quit saying that!

DUWELL. I cain't help it. It rhymes.

DUANE. My boots are soaked.

DUWELL. You think she's in the lake?

DUANE. *(Exasperated.)* I don't know, Duwell. Why don't you call out and ask her?

DUWELL. *(Thinks it's an idea.)* Angellll! Angelll! —

DUANE. SHUT UP, YOU MORON! I wasn't serious! *(Looks at boots.)* Aw, dang it! I went shin deep in mud. Dang it! *(Bends over.)* I need a stick. *(Duane's rear end sticking out. As Duwell looks over him, a light begins to glow. It gets brighter. Duwell is mesmerized.)*

DUWELL. Duane ...

DUANE. *(Still bent over, fussing with boots.)* Hang on a second. This damn mud.

DUWELL. It's ... beautiful.

DUANE. It's mud, Duwell.

DUWELL. I never seen anything like it.

DUANE. You got mud all around your porch, you idiot.

DUWELL. Don't go ... *(Light fades.)*

DUANE. I ain't going. You are. *(Duwell still in a daze. Duane stands.)*

Duwell? DU-WELL! You gonna make that phone call or what?

DUWELL. *(Dreamy.)* Yes. I'll make the call. *(Walks away.)*

DUANE. *(Yelling after him.)* And remember, no details!

DUWELL. *(Robotic.)* No details.

DUANE. Tell him it was a deer, for God's sakes.

DUWELL. Dear ... God ...

DUANE. And don't mention it was us!

DUWELL. It was us. *(Lights off on Duane. Duwell picks up "phone.")* Hello, Sheriff Otis? This is Duwell Early. Me and Duane just shot an angel. That's right. A big beautiful heaven-sent angel. We shot it dead ... I know it ain't in season. But we shot it jus' the same. I'm confessin' my sin. We shot it and it landed smack in Mudder's Lake. *(Lights up on Sandy and Lenny looking at a map.)*

SANDY. Someplace called Mudder's Lake.

LENNY. *(Eating his donuts.)* And once we find them, then what?

SANDY. We give them money.

LENNY. And what do they give us?

SANDY. A photograph. A couple of lies. And our ticket home. You know how it works.

LENNY. Yeah. My last assignment was a woman who said she had Hitler's mustache in a box. We gave her a thousand bucks.

SANDY. And did she *have* Hitler's mustache?

LENNY. She had a mustache. In a box. It had sauerkraut on it.

SANDY. Works for me. *(Chuckle.)*

LENNY. Man, wouldn't that beat all?

SANDY. If that was Hitler's mustache?

LENNY. Nah. If there really was an angel.

SANDY. Why? You have something you want to ask it?

LENNY. An angel? Oh, hell, yeah. Think of the mysteries it could explain. Good. Evil.

SANDY. Riverdance.

LENNY. War. Intelligence.

SANDY. Donald Trump's hair.

LENNY. The Grand Canyon.

SANDY. Velveeta.

LENNY. Big Foot.

SANDY. Dr. Phil.

LENNY. Hey, man. Dr. Phil's my boy. *(Imitating Dr. Phil's southern drawl.)* Get the wax outa your ears, lady. *(Enter Lester, phone to ear, Gator Man Creature trailing him. The creature sits on all fours. Lester*

drops his pants and sits on the creature's back, as if sitting on a toilet.)
LESTER. Get the wax outa your ears, Sandy!
SANDY. *(Lifting cell phone to ear.)* Hello, Lester.
LESTER. Don't look now, but CNN is on your ass.
SANDY. *(To Lenny.)* My ass is on CNN.
LENNY. Why your ass? Why not my ass?
LESTER. This angel story? It's out. Someone's calling everybody.
Cable. Newspapers. *People* Magazine. They're all headed down there.
SANDY. There IS no angel, Lester.
LESTER. I know that. But I'm smarter than those morons.
LENNY. Why your ass?
LESTER. Have you seen anybody from CNN yet?
SANDY. No. If I do, do you want me to shoot them?
LESTER. No, I want you to *beat* them, you burnout! Pay off who-
ever you got to pay off but make sure nobody else sees this thing.
SANDY. What thing?
LESTER. The ANGEL!
SANDY. *(Sighs.)* There is no angel, Lester.
LENNY Get MY ass on CNN!
LESTER. It doesn't matter that there's no angel, Sandy. It only mat-
ters that people *think* there is! And if CNN and *People* Magazine are
chasing it, THEY think there is, and I want to beat those pompous
putzes at their own game — just once! You got that? You hear what
I say? *(Lights off on them, Lights up on Duane and Duwell.)*
DUANE. What'd he say?
DUWELL. Who?
DUANE. WHO? Otis?
DUWELL. He said angels weren't in season.
DUANE. You told Otis about the ANGEL?
DUWELL. Well, not exactly.
DUANE. Thank God.
DUWELL. I told a lot of people.
DUANE. WHAT?
DUWELL. She's a gift to humankind, Duane. People have the
right to know.
DUANE. *(Nervously.)* Duwell? … What … did you … do?
DUWELL. I phoned a few people.
DUANE. How few?
DUWELL. Four few.
DUANE. Four few?

DUWELL. Eight few.

DUANE. EIGHT FEW?

DUWELL. Call it an even dozen.

DUANE. DUWELL, I'm gonna KILL YOU! *(They begin to fight. Wrestling and grabbing. The following is done as they flip and flop atop each other:)*

DUWELL. Lemme go!

DUANE. Damn your mouth!

DUWELL. Don't say damn!

DUANE. Why not!

DUWELL. You'll make God angry!

DUANE. We shot one of his ANGELS, you IDIOT! How much angrier can we make him!?

DUWELL. Maybe he's not mad!

DUANE. No, I'm sure he's THRILLED! Maybe when we get to the gates of Heaven, we can shoot GABRIEL, TOO!

DUWELL. Stop it, Duane!

DUANE. And Peter! And PAUL!

DUWELL. Lemme go!

DUANE. And MARY!

DUWELL. Don't blaspheme!

DUANE. Blaspheme? Oh, Duwell, we went right past blaspheme! We went straight to BUCKSHOT!

DUWELL. It ain't that bad, Duane!

DUANE. NOOO! I'm sure we could have ax-murdered a few apostles!

DUWELL. You don't understand!

DUANE. Why didn't you just go to confession and give the priest your shell casings?

DUWELL; Confession is good for the soul!

DUANE. That's what they tell you in PRISON!

DUWELL. We won't go to prison!

DUANE. Right! We'll be too busy in PURGATORY!

DUWELL. Lemme go!

DUANE. Oh, no! Uh-uh! If I'm going to the devil, I'm taking you with me! And I'm gonna say to him, "Hello, Lucifer. This here's Duwell, the luckiest shot on the face of the earth! He couldn't hit a parked airplane, but he plugged an angel without even looking!"

DUWELL. She ain't dead yet!

DUANE. You're gonna be!

DUWELL. She's only wounded! *(Breaking apart, exhausted.)* She ain't dead yet … I seen her

DUANE. What the hell are you talking about? *(Lights off on them, up on Sandy. He is holding a flashlight, wearing a hooded rain coat.)*

SANDY. *(To Voice.)* They stayed there three days, hiding and beating each other up. I think they were hoping the whole thing would blow over, and they could go home eventually. Like in the Spring.

VOICE. Did they see the angel again?

SANDY. Not exactly. But three days in a swamp is not the best thing for your perspective. Fortunately, we found them first. *(He pulls hood over his head, covering most of his face.)*

DUANE. *(Off-stage.)* Who's there? *(Sandy steps in with flashlight. Lights up on Duane and Duwell, huddled together.)*

SANDY. Hey … Are you guys all right?

DUANE. *(Frightened, whispering.)* What'd I tell you, Duwell? Beezlebub done caught us already.

DUWELL. *(In awe, to Sandy.)* Are you from…? *(He points up.)*

SANDY. Up north.

DUANE. *(To Duwell.)* That's what they're callin' it now?

SANDY. *(A tad confused.)* No. It's always been … up north.

DUWELL. *(Whispering to Duane.)* That's a good sign, ain't it? We're goin' up, instead of down?

DUANE. Don't be a fool, Duwell. He's got a Yankee accent. He HAS to be from hell. *(To Sandy.)* A-hem. What can we do you for, Mister?

SANDY. You men been doing some hunting?

DUANE. Us? No. *(Grabbing the rifles.)* We jus' come out here to settle our differences.

DUWELL. Yup. Yup. Settle our differences.

SANDY. You're gonna shoot one another?

DUANE. Hell, no! We wouldn't shoot one another!

DUWELL. And we wouldn't shoot no angels, neither.

DUANE. *(Under breath.)* SHUT UP YOU MORON!

SANDY. I beg your pardon?

DUWELL. What's it like, Mister?

SANDY. I'm sorry?

DUWELL. What's it like? Up … north?

SANDY. Well, when I left, it was pretty cloudy. *(Duane and Duwell nod at each other hopefully.)*

DUWELL. Clouds. That's good.

SANDY. And crowded.

DUWELL. Of course. Everyone wants to be there.

SANDY. I guess.

DUANE. People dying to get up there, huh?

SANDY. Well. I suppose.

DUANE. I guess it beats the alternative, huh? Where it's … *warm* all the time?

SANDY. You mean the South? Well, I did some time in the south.

DUWELL. You did?

SANDY. Yeah. It wasn't a great experience.

DUWELL. Did it hurt?

SANDY. Hurt?

DUWELL. You know … Fiiiire…?

SANDY. I wasn't fired. I quit.

DUWELL. *(Amazed.)* They let you quit?

SANDY. Well, I had a better offer. Up north.

DUWELL. Wowww.

DUANE. How did you get the better offer?

SANDY. I guess you have to be good.

DUWELL. *(As if lecturing, to Duane.)* You have to be good.

SANDY. Anyhow, listen. I was sent down here to look for a couple of guys. Duane and Duwell?

DUANE. *(Almost simultaneously.)* We don't know 'em —

DUWELL. How did you know our names?

SANDY. So you're —

DUANE. *(Glaring at Duwell.)* We *don't know* them. *(Enter Lenny, eating donuts, cameras over neck, stepping awkwardly, trying to avoid the mud. They all look at his strange walk. He speaks with donuts in mouth.)*

LENNY. Therff's mmmddd efffryvwhrr

DUWELL. Is he from … up north, too?

SANDY. That's right.

DUWELL. Look. They got donuts up there, Duane.

DUANE. Hold on a minute … There's no Crispy Kremes in heaven! *(Lifts rifle.)* Identify yourself, Mister!

LENNY. *(Drops box, puts hands in air, spits out donut.)* Shit! I ain't in Alabama five minutes, I got my hands up.

SANDY. Put the gun down, Mister.

DUWELL. Put it down, Duane.

DUANE. Shut up, Duwell. Don't give 'em my name!

SANDY. You're Duwell?

DUWELL. *(Nodding.)* And he's Duane.

DUANE. Duwell!

DUWELL. C'mon, Duane.

SANDY. Mister, we mean you no harm. We received a phone call.

DUANE. Oh, really? *(Staring at Duwell.)* Which one of the twelve?

SANDY. We're with a newspaper.

DUANE. What newspaper?

SANDY. Actually, it's a tabloid.

DUWELL. You can swallow it?

SANDY. A tabloid. *The Weekly World and Globe.*

DUWELL. *(Thrilled.)* Holy sheet!

DUANE. You gotta be kiddin!

DUWELL. *(Dancing around.)* Holy sheet!

DUANE. Duwell's a big fan.

DUWELL. *The Weekly World and Globe!* Here in our swamp!
(Runs and embraces Sandy.)

SANDY. Yes. *(Squirming.)* Miracles happen.

DUWELL. *(To Duane.)* Miracles happen! *(Grabs paper from pocket.)*
Oh, look! Look! I got your latest one right here. Picked it up at the
Piggly Wiggly. Got the wolf-boy story, And that picture of Lot's wife,
a big pillar of salt, and — Oh! Hey! Whatever happened to that half-
man-half-alligator? Did he ever avenge hisself?

SANDY. *(Beat.)* It's an ongoing investigation.

DUWELL. Holy turd bird, Duane! *The World and Globe!*

DUANE. It's amazing, Duwell.

DUWELL. *(Beat.)* Hey. How come you call it the "weekly" *World
and Globe* but it comes out twice a week.

SANDY. It's a mystery.

DUWELL. Why not call it the bi-weekly *World and Globe?*

SANDY. Well … *(He looks at dumb expression on Duane and
Duwell's faces.)* … they thought if we called it a "bi-weekly," readers might think it was a gay magazine. *(A pause.)*

DUANE. Well that's just silly.

DUWELL. Yeah. Bi ain't gay. Bi is bi.

DUANE. Gay implies sexual activity between a single sex.

DUWELL. Bi-sexuals engage with both sexes.

DUANE. Men and women.

DUWELL. So your readership could go up.

DUANE. Men and women.

DUWELL. Plus "bi-weekly" might attract homosexuals and lesbians.

DUANE. Men and women.

DUWELL. They'd appreciate the spirit.

DUANE. The straight audience might resist.

DUWELL. But most straights are secretly curious about that sort of thing.

DUANE. Two women, one man.

DUWELL. It's a fantasy.

DUANE. For some people.

DUWELL. For some people.

DUANE. Two women, one man!

DUWELL. And how come they call it the *World and Globe*? That's pretty redundant don't you think? World-Globe —

SANDY. OK! OK! I DON'T KNOW WHY THEY CALL IT WHAT THEY CALL IT! *(A beat.)*

DUANE. *(Mumbling.)* Well. You'd think an employee might ask.

DUWELL. I would.

DUANE. Me, too.

LENNY. *(Yells.)* Can I put my hands down now?

SANDY. Sorry, Lenny.

DUWELL. Sorry, Mister. *(Lenny drops hands, grabs camera, starts shooting.)*

DUANE. Hey, what are you doing?

LENNY. I'm making a photo essay. World's smallest redneck.

DUANE. Now hold on there, Mister!

DUWELL. *(Thrilled.)* Our picture's gonna be in the *World and Globe*!

DUANE. Yeah, and then they'll be in the post-office! Gimme that camera, Mister!

LENNY. It's a free country, Duwell.

DUANE. Duane.

DUWELL. I'm Duwell. *(He begins striking serious poses for Lenny.)*

LENNY. And they say Black folks name their kids funny.

SANDY. Which one of you shot the angel?

DUANE. Who said we shot an angel?

DUWELL. They ain't even in season.

SANDY. Well that's what the guy said in the phone call. A duck hunter shot an angel.

DUANE. *(Pointing at Duwell.)* He did!

DUWELL. *(Pointing at Duane.)* He did!

SANDY. And where's this angel now?

DUANE. Why do we have to tell you?

SANDY. It's us or CNN.

DUWELL. The government's involved?

SANDY. CNN? The cable news channel?

DUANE. I ain't got cable on my TV.

SANDY. What about you?

DUWELL. My electricity's shut off.

SANDY. *(Turns to the Voice.)* So much for television causing violence. *(Lights off on everyone but Sandy.)*

VOICE. Did they take you to the angel?

SANDY. They hadn't eaten in three days, and we didn't have enough batteries for the flashlights. So I went for supplies. Duane and Duwell wouldn't come out of the woods because they thought God would strike them down for leaving the scene of an accident. I think they confused religious and secular law there.

VOICE. And then what? *(Lights up on Kansas in store. She is holding two coffee cups, one of which she gives to Sandy as he approaches.)*

KANSAS. And then what?

SANDY. And then Lenny started snapping their pictures. I think he was preparing for the civil suit.

KANSAS. *(Laughing.)* Those boys were never gonna hurt him. They wouldn't hurt a flea.

SANDY. They were shooting at ducks.

KANSAS. They were *trying*. Fact is, there's no place safer for a duck than right in their line of vision.

SANDY. Who told you that?

KANSAS. My mama.

SANDY. Your mama again. She run this place with you?

KANSAS. More like I run it with her. Gasmarts are not my chosen field of study, if you know what I mean.

SANDY. How'd your mom get into this?

KANSAS. She started working here for the previous owner, Maynard McGrady? And she took it over after he died. Wanna hear how he died?

SANDY. Do I have a choice?

KANSAS. *(Animated.)* Well, one day, these two guys pull up and ask Maynard for all the dry ice in the store. Maynard gets a little curious, so he offers to pump the gas for them, but while they're inside, he pops open their trunk and discovers a blindfolded man with a gag in his mouth, and his wrists and ankles all tied up like in them gangster movies? And he figures they're gonna kill him and use the dry ice to keep the body from stinkin'?

SANDY. Something tells me Maynard had cable.

KANSAS. So he lets the air outa their rear tires, and he ties a big old clove of garlic under the bumper! Then as the guys drive off, he sics his dog Cletus to follow the scent, and he calls the cops 'cause he knows the tires are gonna give out and Cletus gotta real good nose for garlic and you can hear him barking from a mile a way. Well! The cops come in, guns a blazin'! Only they find out it was a fraternity prank from the college up in Elmont, and the dry ice was for a keg party, and when they open the trunk, Cletus bites the blindfolded kid in the leg. *(She stops, chuckling at the memory. Long pause.)*

SANDY. *(Finally.)* I don't get it. How did Maynard die?

KANSAS. Oh. He was so embarrassed, he went to Rockville and got hit by a bus.

SANDY. You tell a mean story, kid.

KANSAS. *(Oblivious.)* Yep. And that's when my mama took over the Gasmart. She's behind in her payments a whole bunch now, but I'm not supposed to say anything.

SANDY. I need a couple more boxes of donuts. And some flashlight batteries.

KANSAS. It's not so bad, running a place like this. On occasion, someone interesting comes through. That's what my mama says. You never know who walks in your door, maybe the man of your dreams.

SANDY. Only if he needs gas.

KANSAS. Or donuts.

SANDY. *(Grinning.)* Or donuts. Listen, kid. You're not gonna have any trouble finding the man of your dreams. *(He looks around at the empty store.)* He might have some trouble finding you.

KANSAS. You gonna write a newspaper story about Duane and Duwell?

SANDY. I suppose. It's not every day someone shoots an angel.

KANSAS. Oh, I don't know. People do it all the time.

SANDY. *(Totally lost.)* I gotta get out of the south. *(Lights off on them. Lights up on Lenny and Duane. Duane is pacing nervously.)*

DUANE. So when did you leave the south?

LENNY. Shit, I ain't from down here.

DUANE. *(Off-handedly.)* Oh, you one of them northern boys.

LENNY. *(Beat.)* I ain't any kind of *boy*.

DUANE. Oops. Hey, no offense, Mister. Everybody's a "boy"

32

around here. You know, like, "Hey. You gonna see Omar McGuiggan's boy down in Fayetteville?" Or, "Say, I seen your boy playing football, he's a big-un." It's just an expression.

LENNY. Just an expression. Like "I see everyone the same"?

DUANE. Hell, no, ain't everyone the same! There's morons and idiots and then there's your more intellectual types, like myself.

LENNY. *(Laughing.)* Oh, you the intellectual type.

DUANE. *(Stung.)* Well, go ahead and laugh. Ain't that just like a northern boy. *(Oops.)* Man. Northern man. *(Lenny glares at him. Shakes his head. Sighs.)*

LENNY. And to think, my boss is gonna give you money.

DUANE. *(New interest.)* Money? What fer, money?

LENNY. For your "story."

DUANE. You gonna pay us for shooting an angel?

LENNY. We're gonna pay you so you don't give it to the AP.

DUANE. Aw, we don't talk to the Feds.

LENNY. Yeah. Well. I ain't got the loot. Sandy does.

DUANE. And what do we gotta do for it?

LENNY. Just pose for pictures. And don't talk to nobody else.

DUANE. Well, heck … we can do that.

LENNY. *(Sarcastically.)* I knew that you could. *(Enter Sandy, carrying bags.)*

SANDY. There you are. Damn it, this fog is impossible. All right. I got supplies. *(Takes out donuts for Lenny.)* Here's your donuts.

DUANE. Did you get the jerky?

SANDY. Yes. I got the jerky. Two flavors. *(Looking in bag.)* Beef and … raw beef.

DUANE. Hot damn! Thank you, Mister. *(Duane rips open bag and eats like an animal. Lenny holds his donut.)*

LENNY. *(Watching Duane, mocking.)* Jerky. The official health food of the southern intellectual.

DUANE. *(Glares, then, just as mockingly.)* Dooo-nuts. Official breakfast of Fat Albert!

SANDY. Where's the other one?

DUANE. *(With a mouthful.)* Duwell snout trrraking abee.

SANDY. I beg your pardon?

LENNY. *(Mouth full of donuts.)* He'snooot mrkaing anee.

SANDY. OK. I'll wait for the English translation. *(They both finish at the same time.)*

LENNY and DUANE. He's out taking a pee!

SANDY. Thank you. *(Sound of thunder. They flinch and duck. They slowly back into each other. Thunder continues. Sounds of rain.)*

SANDY. Great. Just what was missing.

LENNY. My cameras are gonna get soaked.

DUWELL. *(Screaming, Offstage.)* Oh, god!

DUANE. Duwell? Where are you?

DUWELL. Oh, dear God!

SANDY. Where'd he go?

LENNY. To take a pee! *(Thunder increases. Lightning, too. Now the sound of plaintive voice, heard earlier, an angel's cry.)*

DUWELL. *(Offstage. Moaning.)* What did we do!

DUANE. Duwell? Come out now!

DUWELL. *What did we do?*

DUANE. He's gone over the edge!

LENNY. He shoulda eaten something.

DUANE. He's dehydrated.

SANDY. He went for a pee! How can he be dehydrated!

DUWELL. FORGIVE US!

DUANE. For what Duwell?

SANDY. Yeah, for WHAT, Duwell?

DUWELL. I HAD MY PANTS DOWN!

SANDY. He had his pants down?

DUANE. Maybe a snake bit his peter!

SANDY. His what?

LENNY. *(Pulling camera close.)* Lester'll buy that for sure!

DUWELL. WHERE IS THE REST?

SANDY. You can rest right here, Duwell.

DUWELL. WHERE IS THE REST?

DUANE. *(Yelling.)* Duwell, did a snake bite your peter?

DUWELL. WHERE IS THE REST?

LENNY. The rest of what?

DUANE. The rest of WHAT, DUWELL? *(Big thunder clap.)*

DUWELL. This! *(Lightning flash brings light up on Duwell, holding up a giant angel's wing. Blackout.)*

End of Act One

ACT TWO

*Darkness. Sound of a song like Clyde McPhatter's "A Lover's Question."** Lights up on Woman and Gator dancing together to the music. After a short while, Gator Man exits and Woman sits down, as if resting between dances. Enter Sandy, watching this. Woman, in dream mode, doesn't acknowledge him.*

VOICE. What is it?

SANDY. Sorry. Just that song.

VOICE. What about it?

SANDY. Nothing. One of those fond memory things.

VOICE. A girl?

SANDY. Isn't that where most fond memories begin?

VOICE. Who was she?

SANDY. Oh, a long time ago. In Birmingham. A late night joint. This was playing on a jukebox. "A Lover's Question." And she ... *(A chuckle.)* she always had a lot of questions.

WOMAN. What was it like? Going to college?

SANDY. *(Half to voice, half to her.)* She was so ... innocent, you know?

WOMAN. What's it like, seeing your name in the newspaper?

SANDY. She made me feel special. They're the worst kind, aren't they? The ones that make you feel special?

WOMAN. What do your friends call you, Mister?

SANDY. *(Turning.)* Sandy.

WOMAN. Do you wanna dance, Sandy? *(Music up. A slow romantic song. They fall into a step. Sandy is awkward, steps on her toes. He breaks away, embarrassed, but she encourages him back. They smile and rejoin. Clearly enjoying each other. They move in closer, then finally, he embraces her hard, as if holding onto a memory. Woman slowly pulls away from him and departs. Music down. A saddened Sandy turns back to the voice.)*

SANDY. Anyhow ... I left you hanging on that story, didn't I?

---

* See Special Note on Songs and Recordings on copyright page.

VOICE. The Angel.

SANDY. Right. What was I talking about? *(Blast of sound and Lights up on final moment of first act. Everyone in place, Duwell holding up the angel wing.)*

DUWELL. THIS! *(They all freeze. Sandy laughs.)*

SANDY. THAT was a moment. I have to admit, even *I* started to wonder at that point.

VOICE. You were surprised?

SANDY. *(Moving around as he speaks.)* Well, it isn't every day someone steps out of the woods with his pants around his ankles holding one half of an angel's flying apparatus. Still, I always figured the whole thing was a hoax.

VOICE. A hoax?

SANDY. Sure. People do it all the time. I oughta know. We specialize in hoaxes at the *World and Globe*. Like the guy who said he found Howard Hughes' will in a hornet's nest. I flew all the way to Utah for that one.

VOICE. It wasn't true?

SANDY. Not unless you spell Hughes H-E-W-S.

VOICE. You don't believe in much, do you?

SANDY. I believe in certain things.

VOICE. Such as?

SANDY. Oh, let's see ... I believe in ketchup on a hamburger but never a hot dog. I believe Yo-Yo Ma's parents should be punished for giving him that name. And I believe — above all else — that everyone has a price. *(He exits. Enter Duane and Duwell, Duwell holding angel wing.)*

DUANE. I'm upping our price, Duwell.

DUWELL. Whatchu mean, Duane?

DUANE. Our price. This here mess you got us into is turning into a bid'ness opportunity.

DUWELL. It was *your* bullet.

DUANE. Quit sayin' that!

DUWELL. But you're a better shot.

DUANE. At ducks!

DUWELL. We ain't never hit a duck.

DUANE. Well, I came closer than you.

DUWELL. *(As he continues exploring the wing, not looking at Duane.)* How do you know?

DUANE. I seen 'em flinch, OK?

DUWELL. You seen a duck flinch?

DUANE. Yeah. Offa MY bullet, not yours.

DUWELL. *(Starting to try the angel wing on his shoulder.)* How do you know it was *your* bullet?

DUANE. 'Cause I know, OK?

DUWELL. How do you know it was a flinch? How do you know it wasn't just scratchin' itself, or rubbin' its eye, or —

DUANE. DAMN YOU, DUWELL! *(Slapping him across the belly, the wing drops.)* TAKE THAT WING OFF! WE AIN'T TRYIN' OUT FOR NO CHRISTMAS PAGEANT HERE! NOW CONCENTRATE ON THE PROBLEM AT HAND!

DUWELL. Eternal damnation?

DUANE. PRICE! This here angel-sightin' business is just like the flea market. There's buyers and sellers.

DUWELL. Which one are we?

DUANE. What?

DUWELL. The buyers or the sellers?

DUANE. Duwell, if they turned Alabama upside down and shook it until everyone with a brain fell out, you'd still be in your kitchen.

DUWELL. *(Pause.)* So are we the buyers or the sellers?

DUANE. We're the *shooters*, Duwell! That makes us a hot commodity.

DUWELL. *(Glumly.)* Yeah. Hot as the devil.

DUANE. Not that kinda hot. Hot like a fishin' license when the river's high! Hot like a Hooters girl in a bar fulla truckers! Now lookie here. Do we *gotta* deal with these two boys from the *World and Globe*?

DUWELL. Whatchu mean?

DUANE. I mean maybe we can do better.

DUWELL. It's the *Weekly World and Globe*, Duane. It don't get no better than that.

DUANE. What about them TV people? The ones sound like they from the government?

DUWELL. What about em?

DUANE. Maybe they'll double the offer for our story!

DUWELL. You said we're doomed.

DUANE. Well, being doomed is *a hell of a story, ain't it?* Damn it, Duwell, if I gotta spend the rest of my days in flames, can't I get me a few toys before I go?

DUWELL. Duane, I don't know.

DUANE. Well, That's the difference between me and you, Duwell. I know and you don't.

DUWELL. Maybe we should tell the world about her.

DUANE. Tell the world?

DUWELL. About the angel. And her goodness. And her purity. Maybe that's our calling, Duane. Maybe that's what we're here on earth for. Maybe we're like … the two wise men. *(Long pause as they look to the heavens and consider this.)*

DUANE. Don't be a fool, Duwell. That's only when a baby is born. *(Lights up on Kansas in store, as Sandy Enters.)*

KANSAS. Baby been born yet?

SANDY. Excuse me?

KANSAS. Your significant other? In the car?

SANDY. Trust me. If that significant other gives birth, the world will know about it.

KANSAS. Will we read it in your newspaper?

SANDY. Ohhhh, yeah. My newspaper's the perfect place.

KANSAS. So whatcha need this time? I'm gonna have to re-order donuts.

SANDY. I just need a few more staples. *(He pulls beer off the shelf, along with snack foods.)*. And I need a favor.

KANSAS. A favor given is a favor promised in return.

SANDY. Sorry?

KANSAS. Somethin' my mama always says. I think where you come from it goes, "There's no such thing as a free lunch."

SANDY. *(Impressed.)* You're right. There isn't. Your mama sounds pretty smart.

KANSAS. And the apple doesn't fall far from the tree.

SANDY. You in school?

KANSAS. One more year of high school. I'm hopin' to go to college.

SANDY. Around here?

KANSAS. Yup. Why?

SANDY. Oh, I don't know. I mean, there might be some better colleges a little further … north.

KANSAS. What makes 'em better? Shakespeare got a New York accent?

SANDY. No, it's just … Never mind. I'm sure the colleges around here are fine.

KANSAS. They are if they can make me smarter. Anyhow, this is my home. Don't you have feelings for your home?

SANDY. I never really had one.

KANSAS. A feeling?

SANDY. A home. I moved around a lot ... Anyhow, about that favor. *(He reaches for his money.)* If some other folks from some other news agencies come through here, asking about this silly angel thing, could you just *(Holds money out.)* sort of forget you ever heard anything about it?

KANSAS. *(She studies the offer.)* Forgettin's easy. It don't require payment.

SANDY. *(Embarrassed.)* Sorry. I'm used to people holding me up. *(Exit Sandy and Kansas. Lights up on Duane, Duwell and Lenny, all exhausted.)*

LENNY. Hold up.

DUANE. What?

LENNY. Let's stop for a minute. *(They plop down. As Lenny does, he sits on something.)* Ow ... shit!

DUWELL. We're out of paper.

DUANE. Use a leaf. *(Lenny reaches beneath him, finds a round shiny tiara.)*

LENNY. Whoa ... mama. I think our angel is a stripper.

DUANE. Whatcha got there? *(He sniffs it.)*

LENNY. *(Staring at him.)* What are you, a Golden Retriever?

DUWELL. *(Stunned.)* It's hers.

DUANE. *(Freaked.)* Oh, no, oh, no ... it's one of them holy crown things ... a teerarium!

LENNY. A tiara, you nitwit. *(Duwell takes the tiara and admires it, tries it on his head.)*

DUANE. Quick! Dig a hole and bury it!

DUWELL. Duane's afraid she might not be the forgivin' kind.

DUANE. *(Angry.)* And Duwell thinks she's gonna meet us at the pearly gates with a medal for marksmanship.

DUWELL. I just said she might not be mad.

DUANE. She's already missing a wing and a crown! How much more has to fall off before she loses her temper?

LENNY. Let's wait here till Sandy gets back.

DUANE. Suits me fine. *(They assume relaxed positions. Duane senses an opening.)* And, uh ... while we have a moment ... My brother and I have been re-considering our situation.

LENNY. Come again? *(Duwell, uncomfortable, tries to hold Duane back, but can't.)*

DUANE. We feel that given the rare nature of our story and the fact that various parties seem to be interested in that there story, that our rumeration should be, as they say in funnencial circles, nac-celerated.

LENNY. Yo, man. I don't speak hillbilly.

DUWELL. Duane wants to greet the devil in a double wide.

DUANE. Shut up, Duwell! Listen, Mister. I'll put it plain as shippin' wrap. We want more money.

LENNY. Oh. In that case — Sandy handles the loot.

DUWELL. Is Sandy the President of the *World and Globe*?

LENNY. *(Chuckle.)* The President? Nah. He writes. Tell you the truth, he's way too talented for our place. I don't know why he stays there.

DUWELL. Well, it's obvious why a man would stay there. You get all them exciting stories! Like the vampire at the Stop and Shop? I was holding my neck the whole time I read that one! And that interview with the *real* Jiminy Cricket? That was fascinatin'.

DUANE. *(Mocking.)* Fascinatin'.

DUWELL. It was! He said the movie exaggerated the whole relationship between him and Pinocchio. That he never hid inside his shirt pocket or nothing like that.

DUANE. *(Stunned.)* Duwell, I swear you was adopted.

LENNY. *(Amused.)* Jiminy Cricket … What was that song? … *(Starts to sing.)* When you get in trouble and you don't know what to do …

DUWELL. *(Joining in.)* Give a little whistle. *(Whistles.)*

LENNY. Give a little whistle. *(Whistles.)*

DUWELL. And always let your conscience be your guide. *(A pause. Duwell smiling and content. Duane flummoxed. Lenny chuckling to himself. Then … turns to Duane:)* And always let your conscience be y —

DUANE. WILL YOU SHUT UP, DUWELL! SHUT UP! SHUT UP! SHUT UP! *(Suddenly, the loud sounds of a helicopter overhead.)*

LENNY. What the hell is that? *(Lights off on them, Lights up on Sandy, on cell phone, with supplies, looks up.)*

SANDY. What the hell is that? *(Light up on Lester, phone to ear, as Gator Man shaves him.)*

LESTER. What the hell is that, Sandy?

SANDY. *(Still looking up, as he continues to walk.)* I think the competition has arrived.

LESTER. Damn it! That's what I was calling about! My snitch at

CNN said they have choppers over some place called Mudder's Lake. So does NBC, CBS, ABC, FOX, and The Animal Planet.

SANDY. The Animal Planet?

LESTER. They were hunting ducks, remember?

SANDY. Oh, right —

LESTER. Up the money, Sandy.

SANDY. Up the money?

LESTER. To the hunters! Huey and Louie? Up the money!

SANDY. How much?

LESTER. I don't know — five thousand. That's gotta be twice their annual income, right?

SANDY. Hard to say. One keeps talking about a double wide.

LESTER. What's that? A fat chick?

SANDY. A trailer.

LESTER. How much they cost?

SANDY. I'm not sure.

LESTER. Well, find out! Do an ad swap.

SANDY. Lester, I'm in a swamp. There aren't many dealerships along the way.

LESTER. And there aren't many employers who will pay you to talk to dimwits! Do your job, Sandy! And get rid of those helicopters!

SANDY. How am I supposed to do that?

LESTER. BUY A GUN! *(Exit Lester and Gator Man. The helicopter noise abruptly stops. Sandy lowers phone.)*

SANDY. *(To Voice.)* Buy a gun, he said. Some career, huh?

VOICE. Tell me more about the girl.

SANDY. But I'm in the middle of the helicopter.

VOICE. Why did you leave her?

SANDY. Is this the character part of the interview? Couldn't I just look at some ink stains?

VOICE. Why did you leave her? *(Enter Woman. She hands Sandy a tie, which he puts on.)*

WOMAN. Why are you leaving?

SANDY. I told you. It's not leaving. It's going someplace else.

WOMAN. It feels the same to me.

SANDY. Sweetie, it's just the business.

WOMAN. The business.

SANDY. If you don't grab the opportunity, it might not come again.

WOMAN. *(Half to herself.)* I was thinking the same thing.

SANDY. As soon as I get settled, you'll come up and visit.

WOMAN. I have to tell you something.

SANDY. What?

WOMAN. When will you come back?

SANDY. It shouldn't be long. Just as soon as I get settled … Hey. Don't look so miserable. We've had a lot of fun.

WOMAN. Fun?

SANDY. You know what I mean. The stuff we did.

WOMAN. The stuff?

SANDY. Yeah.

WOMAN. Like dancing? That stuff?

SANDY. Well, yeah.

WOMAN. Like that place where you bought me the music box? Like the Ferris wheel at the carnival where you threw up? Like the time you tried to kiss me while I was eating spaghetti and I poked you in the nose with my fork? That stuff?

SANDY. Hey, don't do this —

WOMAN. Like skinny-dippin in the reservoir? Like the time I rode you piggyback through the grocery store? Like the bowling —

SANDY. I never really liked the bowling —

WOMAN. Like the birthday cake made out of moon pies? Like the first morning we woke up together and you had that little drool comin' from your mouth? You remember that morning? The one *after* the night we made love for the first time? That *stuff*?

SANDY. Hey. *(He sees she is crying. Tries to comfort her.)* Hey. Look. They do have phones up there. Who knows? Maybe the job won't work out. But I have to try this. You know how important this is to my career. *(He holds her hands.)* You can't miss your chance when it comes, right? *(She nods.)* OK, then.

WOMAN. I have to tell you something.

SANDY. What?

WOMAN. I love you. Don't go.

SANDY. I'll be back soon. *(Sandy slowly steps away, letting go of her hands, which she holds out until the lights fade on Woman.)*

VOICE. Did you see her again?

SANDY. No. No, I didn't.

VOICE. Did you ever regret that?

SANDY. *(Long pause here, a calculated answer.)* No. *(Sandy exits. Lights up on Duane and Duwell, at a small pup tent, Duane carrying the angel's wing and the tiara.)*

DUANE. No, no, no, Duwell! Shut your flapper! I ain't listenin'!

DUWELL. But you can't take money for pieces of an angel.

DUANE. And why not?

DUWELL. They ain't ours to sell.

DUANE. Finders keepers.

DUWELL. I don't think that applies to angels.

DUANE. They done fell off her, OK? Now where's my waders? I may have to float out into Mudder's Lake and find us some more riches, hee-hee! *(He removes his pants to reveal ridiculous boxer shorts. He crawls inside tent, his rear end sticking out.)* They're in here somewhere. *(As he fusses, the glowing light comes up from behind the tent. Duwell is mesmerized.)*

DUWELL. Duane …

DUANE. Hang on, I gotta find my waders.

DUWELL. The Lady's smiling at me …

DUANE. Yep. Lady Luck's gonna be smiling at me, too, once I get that money.

DUWELL. Yes ma'am …

DUANE. Yes *what?*

DUWELL. I understand …

DUANE. Well, it's about time, Duwell. We're gonna be rich.

DUWELL. I will do as you ask …

DUANE. That's music to my ears.

DUWELL. Take me.

DUANE. … Say what?

DUWELL. Take me now.

DUANE. Duwell…?

DUWELL. Lift me up. Let me feel your goodness. *(Duane spins around, holding a gunny sack.)*

DUANE. You gone queer on me, aintcha? I knew it. Too much time in the woods. Like them Deliverance fellows. "Squeal like a pig. Squeal like a pig!" *(Angel light fades.)*

DUWELL. No …

DUANE. *(Dressing fast.)* You're damn right, no! A thousand times no! Go find a farm animal like ever'body else.

DUWELL. I know what I must do.

DUANE. Hey! *(Snapping fingers.)* Duwell! Snap outa your homeoromeo fantasy and gimme a hand with this thing.

DUWELL. I know what I must do.

DUANE. I know what you must do, too. You must help me get the wing inside this gunny sack.

DUWELL. Which wing, Duane?

DUANE. Which wing? Which wing what? *(Thunder clap. Lightning flash. Duwell reaches behind tent, lifts another wing.)* Lord have mercy! You're a better shot than I thought, Duwell!

DUWELL. It wasn't my bullet, Duane.

DUANE. Well it wasn't me! *(To sky.)* IT WASN'T ME! *(More thunder ... lights off on them. Lights up on Lenny.)*

LENNY. Is that you, Sandy? *(Enter Sandy, carrying supplies.)*

SANDY. Yeah. I got enough junk here to keep us fed for ... Hey. Where's the Bobsie Twins?

LENNY. Nac-celeratin' their rumeration.

SANDY. *(Puts down bags.)* Oh ... They been gone long?

LENNY. Long enough that you might want to call Lester. Pry some more cash from his steel-belted wallet.

SANDY. He already offered.

LENNY. Shit. I want a dime from that man, I have to sit outside his office with a cardboard sign and a tin cup.

SANDY. You didn't shoot an angel.

LENNY. If I'da known, I'da shot the Easter Bunny.

SANDY. *(Considering.)* He'd have paid for that.

LENNY. *(Jumping up.)* It's still out there ain't it? ... Where's that rifle? *(They laugh. Sandy sits.)*

SANDY. Lenny. We're in a swamp.

LENNY. Yes, my man. I have noticed.

SANDY. In Alabama.

LENNY. I got that, too.

SANDY. You know, there's this kid back at that Gasmart. She's cute. She thinks you're pregnant, by the way.

LENNY. Hey, if Lester'll pay me for it.

SANDY. But she's smart, you know? Sharp like, like ... any sharp kid in New York.

LENNY. Yeah? And?

SANDY. And, I don't know, you wonder how many other kids are down here like that, kids who, you know, if they got out of Hooterville, would be just as accomplished as some Ivy League brat who was born and bred to it. But instead, what do they do? Work in a Gasmart, marry the boy from high school, pop out a few babies, hang overalls from a clothesline, watch Maury Povich, get their hair done once a year for Christmas?

LENNY. *(Exhales.)* Whoo. Man. You need to take something for that.

SANDY. For what?

LENNY. That bad case of northern superiority.

SANDY. Ach. You know I'm right.

LENNY. No. I know you're a bigot.

SANDY. *(Stung.)* Come on now.

LENNY. What? There's all kind of bigots, my man. Maybe you don't care none about skin color, but that's because you divide people by something else.

SANDY. What?

LENNY. Their brains. A nigger to you is just somebody stupid.

SANDY. Hold on —

LENNY. I'ma tell you somethin', my cab-ridin', Zabar's-eatin, Yankee-rootin, *New York Times* crossword-puzzle-solvin' genius — there's smart people everywhere you go. The smartest woman I ever known come from these parts. She never had no formal education. Had to read in bed at night when her kids were asleep. But that woman was smarter than the next ten Ph.D.'s combined. That woman knew *people.*

SANDY. Your mother.

LENNY. Hell, no! My mother didn't know shit! I'm talking about my grade school principal, Mrs. Helmington. Now, that was one smart woman. She took me aside when I was in sixth grade, I was messin' with some bad kids, and she said, "Leonard, you about to make a choice that's gonna set your course for the rest of your life." And I said, "Aw, come on, Mrs. Helmington, I was just messin' a little bit." And she said, "A little bit? Leonard, take two boats in a harbor. You let one start sailin' a few inches in the wrong direction — just a "little bit" — and before you know it, it's gonna be *miles* off course. You point another boat a few inches in the right direction — just a "little bit" different — and it arrives safe and sound. Children start out as innocent as them boats, she said. Where they end up depends on how they steered — every "little bit." A Southern woman told me that. And I'm still waitin' for anyone in New York City to tell me something smarter.

SANDY. *(Thinks it over.)* You're right. I'm wrong. Southern folks are deep-thinking and pithy.

DUANE. *(Screaming from offstage.)* Duwell, you big Catty Whumpus! I'ma pole-ax your ass!

SANDY. On the other hand … *(Duwell comes running in, arms*

stuffed with two angels wings and the tiara, Duane following right behind him. They chase around Lenny and Sandy.)

DUWELL. We ain't doing it, Duane! It ain't proper!

DUANE. You wouldn't know proper if it bit you in the butt!

DUWELL. You can't sell em!

DUANE. Just watch me!

DUWELL. No, Duane! We gotta give these back!

DUANE. Give 'em back?

DUWELL. Re-attach em!

DUANE. Sure! I'll buy some Elmer's Glue!

DUWELL. That won't work — will it?

DUANE. Damn you, Duwell! Them there's the spoils of war, and I'm selling them to the highest bidder!

DUWELL. She needs these to fly home.

DUANE. She's earthbound now. Let her take a plane like everybody else!

DUWELL. She wants 'em back.

DUANE. And I want a gold-plated toilet plunger — but I ain't got one. What I do got is a bone fidee offer for them souvenirs, and I mean to cash it in.

SANDY. What kind of offer?

DUANE. A bona fidee offer!

DUWELL. We ain't selling nothing, Duane!

SANDY. Who made you an offer?

DUANE. *(Pulling out sheet of paper.)* Them boys in the heleecopters. Dropped it on our heads. Sorry, Mister. But you got competition. See here? "Attention: Duck Hunters. Willing to pay for proof of angel end-titty."

SANDY. *(Rolling his eyes.)* Entity.

DUWELL. *(To Sandy.)* What's that?

SANDY. A being, an existence.

DUANE. Whoo. Good. That titty thing had me spooked.

SANDY. *(Taking paper.)* This came from the helicopter?

DUANE. A bunch of them did, out there in the woods, all over the place, like one a them ticker-tape parades.

LENNY. It's CNN?

SANDY. I don't know. It just says meet them at the clearing. Lenny, you know angels. *(Pointing at wings.)* Which kind is that?

LENNY. *(Peering.)* The dead kind?

DUWELL. Don't say that!

SANDY. *(To Lenny.)* Thanks a lot.

DUANE. *(Grabbing paper.)* I believe this means our price just went up?

DUWELL. No deals, Duane. These things ain't ours. They're hers. And she wants 'em back.

DUANE. And how in fat fart's name would you know that?

DUWELL. BECAUSE SHE TOLD ME! *(Others freeze. Sandy steps away. Lights down on others.)*

SANDY. *(To the Voice.)* She told him. Apparently, Duwell and the angel had some sort of psychic connection — which proves the meek really will inherit the earth.

VOICE. Why him?

SANDY. I don't know. Maybe because he didn't over think it.

VOICE. You mean because he believed?

SANDY. Well, they're the same thing, aren't they? I mean, isn't over thinking the death of belief?

VOICE. How do you mean?

SANDY. Remember all the stuff you were sure about as a kid? Santa Claus? The Tooth Fairy?

VOICE. Yes.

SANDY. Once you started "thinking it through" they went away right?

VOICE. You're saying Duwell believed in the Tooth Fairy?

SANDY. *(Thoughtfully.)* Yeah. Pretty much.

VOICE. And the rest of you?

SANDY. Well, let's just say we had our epiphanies. *(Lights up on others, now sitting around a small campfire, Duane and Duwell eating and drinking. Lenny sprawled as if exhausted. They are noticeably messier. Sandy puts cell phone to his ear, steps to the side.)*

LENNY. Three hours of swamp search and nothing.

DUANE. That's how it is with the huntin' business. Feast or phantom.

DUWELL. *(Nodding.)* Feast or phantom.

LENNY. My cameras are ruined.

SANDY. *(Flipping off phone.)* Well, you boys are getting richer all the time.

DUANE. Say that again?

SANDY. The *Weekly World and Globe* is now prepared to give you eight thousand dollars for exclusive rights.

DUANE. You hear that Duwell! Eight grand for our rights!

DUWELL. You can't buy rights for something that's wrong.

DUANE. Aw, sheep shit!

DUWELL. Well you can't.

DUANE. Y'all excuse my brother. He ain't right. The wheel's still turning, but the hamster died, if you know what I mean.

SANDY. Lester says it's on TV.

LENNY. Already?

SANDY. Cable news. They have a little box with a caption. "Search for an angel."

DUWELL. But they ain't even talked to us yet.

SANDY. Doesn't matter. As soon as a rumor comes along, cable cranks out a banner: "Search for an Angel." "America at War." "Britney Breakup."

DUANE. That's why I ain't got cable.

DUWELL. Who's Britney?

DUANE. Waste of money.

DUWELL. Who's Britney?

DUANE. She's that Princess of England, married to the guy with the big ears.

LENNY. That's why you guys buy the *World and Globe*.

SANDY. Exactly. Get the real news. Right, Duwell?

DUWELL. The real news. Hey, Sandy. Can I ask you something?

SANDY. Sure.

DUWELL. That half-man-half-alligator. Why was he so angry?

LENNY. *(Playfully.)* Yeah, Sandy. Why was he so angry?

SANDY. *(Fumpfing.)* Well ... you see, the original man who was eaten by the alligator? It wasn't his time to go.

DUWELL. It wasn't his time?

DUANE. *(Beat.)* What time was it?

LENNY. Yeah. *(Mimics Duane.)* What time was it?

SANDY. It was ... feeding time for the alligators.

DUWELL. Didn't the man know that?

SANDY. No, he didn't. Because he was ... a tourist.

DUWELL. And did he fall outa the boat — or did the gator jump in?

SANDY. He fell out. He dropped his watch.

LENNY. He dropped his watch?

SANDY. And the gator swallowed it.

DUWELL. Just like Peter Pan.

SANDY. Peter Pan?

DUWELL. When the crocodile swallows the ticking clock.

LENNY. I *knew* I heard this story before!

DUWELL. Tick, tock, tick, tock, tick tock —

DUANE. *(Sarcastic.)* What an amazing coincidence.

SANDY. Anyhow, the man was leaning over, looking for his watch, and he fell in, and the croc swallowed him.

DUWELL. Whole or in chunks?

LENNY. Yeah. Whole or in chunks?

SANDY. In chunks. Which is how his bottom half came to be man and the rest was gator.

DUWELL. Half-man-half-gator.

DUANE. *(A beat.)* Why not the top half?

SANDY. What?

DUANE. The top half's a chunk, too. Why not a gator tail with a human head?

SANDY. Because ... he swallowed the legs first?

LENNY. THAT explains it.

DUANE. Yeah, *that* explains it.

SANDY. And because it wasn't his time, from then on, he haunted the swamp to take revenge ... forever and ... ever ... uh ... Amen.

LENNY. Ah-men. *(A beat.)*

DUWELL. I don't believe it.

SANDY. You don't?

DUANE. Hallelujah!

DUWELL. Nuh-uh. Ain't no such thing as "not being your time." Things just happen. There's a big plan for all of us. And even if you don't understand it when, you know, you get eaten by an alligator who swallowed your watch, that's no reason to terrorize little turtles and fishees. *(Sandy and Lenny, amused, look at Duane.)*

DUANE. Don't look at me! I think our mama dropped him on his head! *(Sound of plaintive cry again, then a chorus of the same. it grows in volume. As they react, waving flashlights, moving around, they eventually will pull into a four-cornered surrounding of the campfire.)*

SANDY. What on earth?

DUANE. It ain't from earth!

DUWELL. *(Calmly.)* She's coming.

LENNY. Sandy?

SANDY. Duwell?

DUANE. She's here to take us!

DUWELL. *(Calmly.)* She won't hurt us.

SANDY. *(Meekly.)* I don't believe in angels.

LENNY. Don't say that NOW! You'll piss 'em off!

DUANE. It's judgment day, fellahs! It's Armagethca!

LENNY. Armagethca?

DUWELL. *(Calm.)* She just wants to tell us something.

SANDY. This isn't happening.

DUANE. *(Shoves the tiara into Lenny's hands.)* Here YOU take it!

LENNY. Leave my ass outa this! *(Drops tiara like grenade.)*

DUANE. Hide the evidence! *(He shoves the wings at Lenny.)*

LENNY. Get that shit off me! *(Throws it away.)*

DUANE. HEATHEN!

LENNY. REDNECK!

DUWELL. She wants to tell us something. *(As they yell, Duwell leans over, taking the wing as if he knows what to do with it; the angelic voices mix with the growing sound of helicopters.)*

DUANE. It's the government! Say your prayers!

DUWELL. She's come for something.

SANDY. What's she coming for Duwell? *(Duwell holds the wing up.)*

DUANE. Our father, who art in Heaven, it wasn't my bullet —

LENNY. I definitely ain't getting paid enough!

DUANE. It was Duwell! It was Duwell!

DUWELL. *(To Duane.)* It wasn't me.

DUANE. *(To sky.)* It wasn't me!

LENNY. It wasn't me!

SANDY. It can't be …

DUANE. It sure as shit is!

DUWELL. *(Holding up wings.)* Here's your wings!

DUANE. *(Trying to grab them back.)* That's our insurance!

DUWELL. Here, Angel!

DUANE. That's my double wide! *(The light is now near blinding. The noise at peak levels. Lighting. Thunder. As they are all mesmerized by this, from corner of stage, Woman appears.)*

WOMAN. I have to tell you something. *(Sandy is the only one who notices her.)*

SANDY. What did you say…?

WOMAN. I have to tell you something. *(Sandy steps in her direction. She moves back.)*

SANDY. What? Wait! Don't go! What did you have to tell me? — *(Thunder clap! Lights off on everyone but Sandy as a showering of paper explodes from above. Sandy, looks up as paper rains down on him. Eventually, he picks up a piece. Reading:)* Will double your best offer for Angel entity. *(A beat. Quiet.)*

VOICE. That's all it was? A news helicopter?

SANDY. I wouldn't say that.

VOICE. Did you see the angel?

SANDY. I wouldn't say that either.

VOICE. What did you see?

SANDY. After that? It was more like what we *didn't* see. The wings were gone. The tiara was gone. And Duwell was gone.

VOICE. Where did he go? *(Lights up on others.)*

LENNY. Where did he go?

DUANE. He was swallowed by the light!

SANDY. He was here a second ago.

DUANE. It's just like them alien stories!

SANDY. I *write* those alien stories.

DUANE. Them four-headed bastards! I bet they're making him have sex with them right now!

LENNY. I'd like a picture of *that!*

SANDY. There's an explanation for this.

DUANE. MY SWEET, SIMPLE BROTHER! HE WAS SWAL-LOWED BY THE LIGHT!

LENNY. Not quite swallowed.

SANDY. Come again?

LENNY. There are footprints leading off that way.

DUANE. He's alive? Oh thank *God!* ... I'ma kill that two-timer!

SANDY. Which way do those tracks lead, Duane?

DUANE. Out to the road. DANG! Duwell's cutting himself a better deal!

LENNY. Your brother don't strike me as a deal cutter.

DUANE. Money makes men do strange things, Mister. Read your Bible. Jacob and his brother, Hee Haw? Sold his birthright for a bowl of grits?

LENNY. That must be the southern translation.

SANDY. Why don't we fan out? *(Lights up on Lester and Gator/Man in office. Lester is pacing with the phone to his ear.)*

LESTER. Why doesn't he answer?! Damn it! Remind me to cancel this cell phone service! It sucks! Why don't I have any pictures yet? Remind me to fire Lumpy! He sucks! This whole situation sucks! *(As if looking at TV.)* ... Aw, aw, look at that TV! Look at that! Helicopters over a swamp! "Search For An Angel" ... EXCLUSIVE!

MY ASS! ... Oh, NO ... Is that? ... Is that Wolf Blitzer? On MY Story? ... Is there no justice! Dammit dammit-dammit-Sandy! ANSWER ME!" *(Lights up on Lenny and Duane, walking with flashlights, as if making way through a storm. Cricket sounds. Rain sounds.)*

DUANE. *(Gently at first.)* Answer me, Duwell. Come onnn, your brother's worried about you *(Sudden switch in tone.)* You little chickenshit. I'm gonna slap you so hard it'll change your politics!

LENNY. Why you so hard on your brother, man? He don't do nothin' to you.

DUANE. Stay out of it, you pagan. I'm the older brother. It's my *job* to kick the shit outa him ... *(Softening voice.)* Come onnn, Duuuu-well, those nice men from the *World and Globe* brought Jiminy Cricket with 'em!

LENNY. There you go again, treating him like a fool.

DUANE. Shut your pie hole. I raise that boy since we was youngun's. Daddy ran out. Mama died. Heck, I schooled Duwell myself.

LENNY. That shows.

DUANE. Look Mister. I ain't got nothin' 'gainst you or your kind. Never have. Just don't like people assumin' nothin' 'bout me 'cause how I look or talk. *(Lenny thinks this over.)*

LENNY. *(More softly.)* Me, neither. *(Wail of Angel Voice, haunting, they both freeze.)*

DUANE. Duwell! Stop playin' around! I know that's you! If that was an angel, I'd hear some harps. *(Sound of harps.)*

DUANE and LENNY. Oh, shit. *(They drop to their knees as light comes up. Angel Voice continues. More harps. Lenny keeps shooting, but lowers his camera in awe as light increases.)*

LENNY. Oh my ... Lord.

DUANE. *(Fast.)* It wasn't me, Miss! I didn't shoot ya. I, I, I can't even shoot that good! I been telling Duwell he's the bad shooter but it's me, honest to God! I mean, swear to Jesus! I mean, for Christ's sake! —

LENNY. SHUT UP, DUANE! *(Looking up.)* I'm not *with* him!

DUANE. OK! IT *WAS* ME! I THOUGHT YOU WERE A DUCK! I JUST WANTED TO KILL *SOMETHING* BEFORE I DIED! ... That didn't come out right. *(As the noise increases, they join voices:)*

LENNY. *Whoa-whoa-whoa-whoa-whoa-whoa!*

DUANE. *Whoa-whoa-whoa-whoa-whoa! (Sudden blackness. Silence. Lights up slowly on Duwell, who is sitting in the tree, holding his rifle.*

He is in his long john underwear. Pale looking, but calm.)
DUWELL. *(Singing softly.)* Give a little whistle *(Whistles.)* … give a little whistle … *(Whistle.)* … And always let your … *(Sandy enters, hood up, wet from rain. Duwell stops.)*
SANDY. Duwell? Is that you up there?
DUWELL. Thank you, Sandy.
SANDY. For what?
DUWELL. For looking for me.
SANDY. Duwell. You've been gone for hours. Your brother thinks you're scamming a deal behind his back …
DUWELL. My brother's a good man, Sandy. He just gets confused some times.
SANDY. Duwell. You OK?
DUWELL. Oh, yes. There was something I had to do, but now there's something else I have to do.
SANDY. Well, come on back with me now and we'll do it together.
DUWELL. What I need to do, I can do right here.
SANDY. Duwell, you're in a tree … in your underwear. The only thing you can do right here is build a nest.
DUWELL. You're a good man, too, Sandy. Deep down, I reckon.
SANDY. Thank you, Duwell.
DUWELL. And you know a lot of big things.
SANDY. Well —
DUWELL. But sometimes, knowing all the big things makes you miss some of the small ones.
SANDY. Duwell, I think your brother is negotiating with Barbra Walters by now —
DUWELL. I have to tell you something. *(A beat.)*
SANDY. What did you say? *(Light up on Woman.)*
WOMAN. I have to tell you something.
DUWELL. She was driving home tonight. It was dark. It was raining.
SANDY. Who are you talking about?
WOMAN. When are you coming back?
DUWELL. There was an animal in the road. *She tried to stop. It was an accident.* It was nobody's fault.
SANDY. Who are you talking about?
DUWELL. She's at the hospital right now. But it's too late. She died.
SANDY. *(Nervous.)* Duwell. Come down. You're scaring me.
WOMAN. I don't want you to go.

53

DUWELL. You've been given a gift, Sandy. An undiscovered story. Like the wolf man at the Piggly Wiggly. Only this one's true *(Removes gun from holster.)*

SANDY. Duwell, put the gun down.

WOMAN. I have to tell you something.

DUWELL. *(His hold on the gun grows more menacing.)* She had to tell you something.

SANDY. Put the gun down now, Duwell.

DUWELL. I never really did like huntin', you know?

WOMAN. I have to tell you something.

DUWELL. *(Pointing gun in Sandy's direction.)* It wasn't me that shot the angel, Sandy.

SANDY. I believe you!

DUWELL. It wasn't Duane.

SANDY. Fine! Fine!

DUWELL. It was you. *(He holds rifle as if he might shoot.)*

SANDY. Whoa! Hold on, hold on, hold on! I didn't shoot anything! I've never fired a gun in my life!

DUWELL. It don't take bullets to shoot an angel, Sandy. People do it every day.

SANDY. I don't understand.

DUWELL. They give up. They quit on *themselves*. They turn their back on a true love. *(As if firing.)* Pow. *(Lowers gun.)* It don't take a gun, Sandy. Sometimes all you got to do to shoot your angels is walk away. *(A beat.)*

WOMAN. I have to tell you something.

DUWELL. She had to tell you something.

SANDY. *(Slowly getting it.)* She had to tell me something.

DUWELL. But you never came back.

SANDY. I never came back …

DUWELL. She needs you now.

SANDY. But you said she's gone. You said I can't help her.

DUWELL. You can't. But you can help your daughter.

SANDY. I don't have a daughter.

DUWELL. She needs her daddy now. *(Lights up on Kansas at store, crying, head in hands. Sandy looks.)*

SANDY. My … daughter?

DUWELL. Go on. *(Sandy moves a step towards store, then steps back.)*

SANDY. You talked to the angel? She told you all of this?

DUWELL. Talking to angels ain't that hard. Even a feller from up

54

north can do it.

SANDY. *(Moves away again, then back.)* Wait, Duwell ... how are you gonna —

DUWELL. Don't worry about me, Sandy. I can get home from here.

SANDY. *(To Voice now, lights off on Duwell.)* I had a daughter. Do you understand? ... I had a *daughter* ... She never told me. *(He moves into the store. Lights up on Kansas, sitting, weeping. Her mother, the Woman, is behind her, holding her, like a comforting ghost.)* Kansas? ... I saw the light on ... *(Kansas lifts up. Tries to wipe her tears away. The Woman slides to behind Sandy.)* I heard what happened. I'm ... so sorry ...

KANSAS. *(Crying.)* You heard?

SANDY. Um ... someone ... told me.

KANSAS. I didn't know where else to go ... At the hospital, they said there was a deer in the road, people had been driving over it ... the rain ... the road, it was so wet ... *when she tried to stop* ...

SANDY. It'll be all right, kid ... *(From behind, the Woman nudges him in his daughter's direction, ghost-like. He moves awkwardly to Kansas. Puts one hand on her shoulder, then takes it back.)*

KANSAS. I want my mama ... *Please,* Mister, don't write nothing bad about *her* ... They said it couldn't be helped. She didn't mean to hurt nobody ...

SANDY. *(Confused.)* She didn't hurt anybo —

KANSAS. Duwell Early. That poor man. He was just trying to get that deer off the road ...

SANDY. Duwell Early?

KANSAS. — when it happened ... it was so fast ... My mama liked Duwell, she did, she said he was like a child.

SANDY. Duwell Early's fine ... I just ... talked to him.

KANSAS. What?

SANDY. *(It hits him full on.)* " ... Even a fellah from up north can do it."

KANSAS. *(Softly.)* ... What am I gonna do, Mister? ... I don't have nobody else ...

SANDY. Kansas ... *(She abruptly runs into his arms. He is stunned, tries to be comforting.)* ... Let me drive you home ... I have to tell you something ... *(Sandy walks her off, stage right. He looks after her as she goes. The Woman smiles, then exits stage left. Enter the man behind the Voice, the bank loan officer. He walks past Sandy as if inspecting something, running his fingers along it, looking around.*

Sandy still looks where Kansas departed.)

LOAN OFFICER. It'll need work.

SANDY. I know.

LOAN OFFICER. A lot of work.

SANDY. *(Turning.)* But it's doable, right?

LOAN OFFICER. Sandy —

SANDY. I know, I know, I haven't got any "retail experience," but it's a Gasmart, you know? It sort of runs itself. People come here for gas. People come here for food — and get gas. I have all the ledgers. And if you and your bank can just see your way to this loan, I'm sure between me and my daughter we can make this thing work … This is her home, you know? And maybe it's mine, too. With your help.

LOAN OFFICER. And you'd be happy here?

SANDY. *(Exhale.)* Well. I have someone who needs me now. And when I look at her she reminds me that … I actually *was* happy here, once … It's funny. I write crap. I *did* write crap. But a true story can be more amazing than anything you make up. *(Sandy thinks on this for a moment.)*

LOAN OFFICER. Come in tomorrow at ten A.M. We'll go over the papers.

SANDY. *(Very grateful, shaking his hand.)* Thank you! Thank you, sir. Thank you. *(Loan Officer goes to leave. Stops. Turns.)*

LOAN OFFICER. Sandy?

SANDY. Mm?

LOAN OFFICER. Did the *World and Globe* ever print that story? *(Lights up on Lester, with edition of* The World and Globe *splayed in front of him. Lenny is in opposite chair, counting money and putting it in an envelope. Gator Man sits between them in chair, with coffee cup.)*

SANDY. Ohhhh, yeah. It was a big seller. They didn't even need me! They made it all up. Lester bought every picture Lenny had. And Lenny gave the money to Duane Early — as a downpayment on a double wide. They ran it three weeks in a row: One week it was "Duck Hunter Shoots Angel!" Then "Duck Hunter Taken by Angel!" And then, for good measure, "Duck Hunter Has Sex with Princess Di." Hey. It's what they do. *(Sandy exits.)*

LENNY. Later, Lester. *(Wags envelope happily.)* See ya, Phil. *(Lenny exits. Lester tosses paper on desk. Walks off and yells back over his shoulder.)* Go home, Phil. Take the costume off. We're done with that story. *(Lester exits. Music up. The opening notes of a song like "Lover's Question" begin. Gator Man lowers his head. Puts down coffee cup. Stands. Looks both ways, then looks straight at audience. He removes his jacket, revealing two giant angels' wings. Then he pulls off the Gator head, revealing Duwell. He smiles, turns his back, throws his hands up into a beam of light from above. Black out.)*

End of Play

PROPERTY LIST

Book
Coffee cups
Dictionary
Tabloid newspaper
Envelope
Rifles
Knapsacks
White feather
Telephone
Papers on desk
Small cake with birthday candle
Wad of bills (money)
Cellphone
Flashlight
Hooded raincoat
News photographer's cameras
Donuts
Beef jerky
2 giant angel wings
Beers
Snack foods
Tiara
Man's tie
Pup tent
Gunny sack
Sheets of paper

SOUND EFFECTS

Car horn
Sounds of rain
Blast of sound
Helicopter
Campfire
Showering of sheets of paper
Harps

NEW PLAYS

★ **MOTHERHOOD OUT LOUD by Leslie Ayvazian, Brooke Berman, David Cale, Jessica Goldberg, Beth Henley, Lameece Issaq, Claire LaZebnik, Lisa Loomer, Michele Lowe, Marco Pennette, Theresa Rebeck, Luanne Rice, Annie Weisman and Cheryl L. West, conceived by Susan R. Rose and Joan Stein.** When entrusting the subject of motherhood to such a dazzling collection of celebrated American writers, what results is a joyous, moving, hilarious, and altogether thrilling theatrical event. "Never fails to strike both the funny bone and the heart." –*BackStage.* "Packed with wisdom, laughter, and plenty of wry surprises." –*TheaterMania.* [1M, 3W] ISBN: 978-0-8222-2589-8

★ **COCK by Mike Bartlett.** When John takes a break from his boyfriend, he accidentally meets the girl of his dreams. Filled with guilt and indecision, he decides there is only one way to straighten this out. "[A] brilliant and blackly hilarious feat of provocation." –*Independent.* "A smart, prickly and rewarding view of sexual and emotional confusion." –*Evening Standard.* [3M, 1W] ISBN: 978-0-8222-2766-3

★ **F. Scott Fitzgerald's THE GREAT GATSBY adapted for the stage by Simon Levy.** Jay Gatsby, a self-made millionaire, passionately pursues the elusive Daisy Buchanan. Nick Carraway, a young newcomer to Long Island, is drawn into their world of obsession, greed and danger. "Levy's combination of narration, dialogue and action delivers most of what is best in the novel." –*Seattle Post-Intelligencer.* "A beautifully crafted interpretation of the 1925 novel which defined the Jazz Age." –*London Free Press.* [5M, 4W] ISBN: 978-0-8222-2727-4

★ **LONELY, I'M NOT by Paul Weitz.** At an age when most people are discovering what they want to do with their lives, Porter has been married and divorced, earned seven figures as a corporate "ninja," and had a nervous breakdown. It's been four years since he's had a job or a date, and he's decided to give life another shot. "Critic's pick!" –*NY Times.* "An enjoyable ride." –*NY Daily News.* [3M, 3W] ISBN: 978-0-8222-2734-2

★ **ASUNCION by Jesse Eisenberg.** Edgar and Vinny are not racist. In fact, Edgar maintains a blog condemning American imperialism, and Vinny is three-quarters into a Ph.D. in Black Studies. When Asuncion becomes their new roommate, the boys have a perfect opportunity to demonstrate how open-minded they truly are. "Mr. Eisenberg writes lively dialogue that strikes plenty of comic sparks." –*NY Times.* "An almost ridiculously enjoyable portrait of slacker trauma among would-be intellectuals." –*Newsday.* [2M, 2W] ISBN: 978-0-8222-2630-7

DRAMATISTS PLAY SERVICE, INC.
440 Park Avenue South, New York, NY 10016 212-683-8960 Fax 212-213-1539
postmaster@dramatists.com www.dramatists.com

NEW PLAYS

★ **THE PICTURE OF DORIAN GRAY by Roberto Aguirre-Sacasa, based on the novel by Oscar Wilde.** Preternaturally handsome Dorian Gray has his portrait painted by his college classmate Basil Hallwood. When their mutual friend Henry Wotton offers to include it in a show, Dorian makes a fateful wish—that his portrait should grow old instead of him—and strikes an unspeakable bargain with the devil. [5M, 2W] ISBN: 978-0-8222-2590-4

★ **THE LYONS by Nicky Silver.** As Ben Lyons lies dying, it becomes clear that he and his wife have been at war for many years, and his impending demise has brought no relief. When they're joined by their children all efforts at a sentimental goodbye to the dying patriarch are soon abandoned. "Hilariously frank, clear-sighted, compassionate and forgiving." –*NY Times.* "Mordant, dark and rich." –*Associated Press.* [3M, 3W] ISBN: 978-0-8222-2659-8

★ **STANDING ON CEREMONY by Mo Gaffney, Jordan Harrison, Moisés Kaufman, Neil LaBute, Wendy MacLeod, José Rivera, Paul Rudnick, and Doug Wright, conceived by Brian Shnipper.** Witty, warm and occasionally wacky, these plays are vows to the blessings of equality, the universal challenges of relationships and the often hilarious power of love. "CEREMONY puts a human face on a hot-button issue and delivers laughter and tears rather than propaganda." –*BackStage.* [3M, 3W] ISBN: 978-0-8222-2654-3

★ **ONE ARM by Moisés Kaufman, based on the short story and screenplay by Tennessee Williams.** Ollie joins the Navy and becomes the lightweight boxing champion of the Pacific Fleet. Soon after, he loses his arm in a car accident, and he turns to hustling to survive. "[A] fast, fierce, brutally beautiful stage adaptation." –*NY Magazine.* "A fascinatingly lurid, provocative and fatalistic piece of theater." –*Variety.* [7M, 1W] ISBN: 978-0-8222-2564-5

★ **AN ILIAD by Lisa Peterson and Denis O'Hare.** A modern-day retelling of Homer's classic. Poetry and humor, the ancient tale of the Trojan War and the modern world collide in this captivating theatrical experience. "Shocking, glorious, primal and deeply satisfying." –*Time Out NY.* "Explosive, altogether breathtaking." –*Chicago Sun-Times.* [1M] ISBN: 978-0-8222-2687-1

★ **THE COLUMNIST by David Auburn.** At the height of the Cold War, Joe Alsop is the nation's most influential journalist, beloved, feared and courted by the Washington world. But as the '60s dawn and America undergoes dizzying change, the intense political dramas Joe is embroiled in become deeply personal as well. "Intensely satisfying." –*Bloomberg News.* [5M, 2W] ISBN: 978-0-8222-2699-4

DRAMATISTS PLAY SERVICE, INC.
440 Park Avenue South, New York, NY 10016 212-683-8960 Fax 212-213-1539
postmaster@dramatists.com www.dramatists.com

NEW PLAYS

★ **BENGAL TIGER AT THE BAGHDAD ZOO by Rajiv Joseph.** The lives of two American Marines and an Iraqi translator are forever changed by an encounter with a quick-witted tiger who haunts the streets of war-torn Baghdad. "[A] boldly imagined, harrowing and surprisingly funny drama." –*NY Times.* "Tragic yet darkly comic and highly imaginative." –*CurtainUp.* [5M, 2W] ISBN: 978-0-8222-2565-2

★ **THE PITMEN PAINTERS by Lee Hall, inspired by a book by William Feaver.** Based on the triumphant true story, a group of British miners discover a new way to express themselves and unexpectedly become art-world sensations. "Excitingly ambiguous, in-the-moment theater." –*NY Times.* "Heartfelt, moving and deeply politicized." –*Chicago Tribune.* [5M, 2W] ISBN: 978-0-8222-2507-2

★ **RELATIVELY SPEAKING by Ethan Coen, Elaine May and Woody Allen.** In TALKING CURE, Ethan Coen uncovers the sort of insanity that can only come from family. Elaine May explores the hilarity of passing in GEORGE IS DEAD. In HONEYMOON MOTEL, Woody Allen invites you to the sort of wedding day you won't forget. "Firecracker funny." –*NY Times.* "A rollicking good time." –*New Yorker.* [8M, 7W] ISBN: 978-0-8222-2394-8

★ **SONS OF THE PROPHET by Stephen Karam.** If to live is to suffer, then Joseph Douaihy is more alive than most. With unexplained chronic pain and the fate of his reeling family on his shoulders, Joseph's health, sanity, and insurance premium are on the line. "Explosively funny." –*NY Times.* "At once deep, deft and beautifully made." –*New Yorker.* [5M, 3W] ISBN: 978-0-8222-2597-3

★ **THE MOUNTAINTOP by Katori Hall.** A gripping reimagination of events the night before the assassination of the civil rights leader Dr. Martin Luther King, Jr. "An ominous electricity crackles through the opening moments." –*NY Times.* "[A] thrilling, wild, provocative flight of magical realism." –*Associated Press.* "Crackles with theatricality and a humanity more moving than sainthood." –*NY Newsday.* [1M, 1W] ISBN: 978-0-8222-2603-1

★ **ALL NEW PEOPLE by Zach Braff.** Charlie is 35, heartbroken, and just wants some time away from the rest of the world. Long Beach Island seems to be the perfect escape until his solitude is interrupted by a motley parade of misfits who show up and change his plans. "Consistently and sometimes sensationally funny." –*NY Times.* "A morbidly funny play about the trendy new existential condition of being young, adorable, and miserable." –*Variety.* [2M, 2W] ISBN: 978-0-8222-2562-1

DRAMATISTS PLAY SERVICE, INC.
440 Park Avenue South, New York, NY 10016 212-683-8960 Fax 212-213-1539
postmaster@dramatists.com www.dramatists.com

NEW PLAYS

★ **CLYBOURNE PARK by Bruce Norris.** WINNER OF THE 2011 PULITZER PRIZE AND 2012 TONY AWARD. Act One takes place in 1959 as community leaders try to stop the sale of a home to a black family. Act Two is set in the same house in the present day as the now predominantly African-American neighborhood battles to hold its ground. "Vital, sharp-witted and ferociously smart." –*NY Times.* "A theatrical treasure…Indisputably, uproariously funny." –*Entertainment Weekly.* [4M, 3W] ISBN: 978-0-8222-2697-0

★ **WATER BY THE SPOONFUL by Quiara Alegría Hudes.** WINNER OF THE 2012 PULITZER PRIZE. A Puerto Rican veteran is surrounded by the North Philadelphia demons he tried to escape in the service. "This is a very funny, warm, and yes uplifting play." –*Hartford Courant.* "The play is a combination poem, prayer and app on how to cope in an age of uncertainty, speed and chaos." –*Variety.* [4M, 3W] ISBN: 978-0-8222-2716-8

★ **RED by John Logan.** WINNER OF THE 2010 TONY AWARD. Mark Rothko has just landed the biggest commission in the history of modern art. But when his young assistant, Ken, gains the confidence to challenge him, Rothko faces the agonizing possibility that his crowning achievement could also become his undoing. "Intense and exciting." –*NY Times.* "Smart, eloquent entertainment." –*New Yorker.* [2M] ISBN: 978-0-8222-2483-9

★ **VENUS IN FUR by David Ives.** Thomas, a beleaguered playwright/director, is desperate to find an actress to play Vanda, the female lead in his adaptation of the classic sadomasochistic tale *Venus in Fur.* "Ninety minutes of good, kinky fun." –*NY Times.* "A fast-paced journey into one man's entrapment by a clever, vengeful female." –*Associated Press.* [1M, 1W] ISBN: 978-0-8222-2603-1

★ **OTHER DESERT CITIES by Jon Robin Baitz.** Brooke returns home to Palm Springs after a six-year absence and announces that she is about to publish a memoir dredging up a pivotal and tragic event in the family's history—a wound they don't want reopened. "Leaves you feeling both moved and gratifyingly sated." –*NY Times.* "A genuine pleasure." –*NY Post.* [2M, 3W] ISBN: 978-0-8222-2605-5

★ **TRIBES by Nina Raine.** Billy was born deaf into a hearing family and adapts brilliantly to his family's unconventional ways, but it's not until he meets Sylvia, a young woman on the brink of deafness, that he finally understands what it means to be understood. "A smart, lively play." –*NY Times.* "[A] bright and boldly provocative drama." –*Associated Press.* [3M, 2W] ISBN: 978-0-8222-2751-9

DRAMATISTS PLAY SERVICE, INC.
440 Park Avenue South, New York, NY 10016 212-683-8960 Fax 212-213-1539
postmaster@dramatists.com   www.dramatists.com